THE
WORKPLACE
WRITER'S
PROCESS

A Guide to Getting the Job Done

Anne H. Janzer

THE WORKPLACE WRITER'S PROCESS
A GUIDE TO GETTING THE JOB DONE
COPYRIGHT © 2017 ANNE H. JANZER

CUESTA PARK CONSULTING
MOUNTAIN VIEW, CA

PRINTED IN THE UNITED STATES OF AMERICA

ISBN-13: 978-0-9864062-7-0

PRAISE FOR
THE WORKPLACE WRITER'S PROCESS

"If you write for an organization, I want to introduce you to your new best friend. Anne Janzer's *The Workplace Writer's Process* will become your go-to guide as you navigate the challenging waters of getting great content produced—from first ideas all the way through publication."

Pamela Wilson
Author, *Master Content Marketing*
Founder, Big Brand System

"You might think the modern workplace interferes with the contemplative work of writing. But Janzer shows business writing is a team sport. Rethink your approach to business writing with the practices in this book."

David Burkus
Author, *Under New Management*

"Anne's latest book is chock full of practical advice for people who need to write as part of their job. She focuses on the stuff they don't teach you in writing classes, covering topics like planning and scoping writing projects, collaborating effectively, utilizing reviewers to deliver what you need, tuning out workplace distractions, and so much more. As someone who works in the tech industry, I especially appreciated Anne's occasional analogies between the writing process and software engineering best practices. If you're being asked to do more writing as part of your job, check out this book!"

Karen Catlin

Advocate for Women in Tech

Coauthor, *Present! A Techie's Guide to Public Speaking*

"Anne Janzer has done it again. She's taken the mysterious, elusive art of writing and outlined a series of tips, processes, and helpful hints that make writing accessible to the mere mortals amongst us. This book is an excellent reference tool that should be at the fingertips of everyone who includes the creation of content in their job description. Don't start your next writing project without it!"

Linda Popky

Strategic marketing expert, writing coach/editor

Author, *Marketing Above the Noise*

"Smooth reading. Anne Janzer managed to present fresh insights and perspectives new to me after 25+ years of successful writing, marketing, and book coaching."

Roger C. Parker

NY Times-recommended design author

Top-performing blogger, Content Marketing Institute

Contents

Introduction:
The Workplace Writer

What would happen to your career if you did *more* writing, creating content that consistently fulfills its objectives? What if you could complete this work efficiently, without doing less of the other projects you are paid to do? Would you become more valuable in your organization and visible in the world beyond?

Your professional, online identity is clothed in written words. The quality and quantity of those words exert a direct and powerful influence on your career. You owe it to yourself to figure out how to become more effective as a writer in the workplace.

You may not consider yourself a writer. One friend of mine with an engineering background has worked as a technical writer for many years. She tells me, "I'm not a *writer* writer."

If writing is *any* part of your job and you are paid to put thoughts into words, you're a writer. Maybe you draft plans or proposals for your team. You might create operational documents for regulators or partners, or content for customers, prospects, the media, or investors.

If writing effectiveness contributes to your job performance, you are a writer.

The more important question is this: What kind of writer are you?

A Field Guide to Writers in the Workplace

The typical office is filled with people writing emails, project plans, reports, assessments, etc. Despite the variety of work, at a high level everyone is doing something similar: assembling thoughts into written form to share with others.

People approach writing tasks with varying mindsets.

- *Inadvertent writers* create written works as a by-product of their jobs, but do not pay much attention to the process. As a result, their projects sometimes go astray. They may resent the time that writing takes away from other responsibilities.

- *Unproductive writers* want to write, but cannot find the time to start projects or to finish them to their satisfaction. Writing ends up at the bottom of their to-do lists.

- *Aspirational writers* wait for the perfect time to start writing. It's always just around the corner.

- *Reluctant writers* don't feel comfortable in the role. In meetings, reluctant writers shrink down and avoid eye contact when someone asks for a blog post, hoping to remain unnoticed.

- *Frustrated writers* struggle getting their projects through to completion, or feel that nobody values or uses the content they create.
- *Overburdened writers* take on all the writing-related tasks for their teams. They become indispensable in this role, unable to free themselves to do other work.

Do any of these types sound familiar? You may have filled one or more of those roles in the course of your career so far.

There's one more model to consider: the *successful, valued writer*. These individuals contribute meaningful content to the business. They leave a trail of completed work, balancing the writing with other responsibilities, and are recognized for their ability to get the job done. Their projects sail through approvals. Others want to collaborate with them.

Successful, valued writers don't always fit our preconceptions of what a writer looks like. They may not have majored in English or writing in college. Perhaps they work as engineers, scientists, project managers, or financial analysts. Writing is another skill that increases their worth in the workplace.

Where do you fit in this field guide to workplace writers?

- Are you a reluctant writer? Consider increasing your visibility and value by stepping up and taking on writing tasks.
- Are you frustrated or overburdened writer? Learn how to complete more projects with less time and effort.
- Are you an aspiring writer? Learn how to plan and scope your projects, and then get started.

You can learn the practices of successful, valued writers, and the best time to start is now.

Writing Matters, More Than Ever

Whether your work reaches an internal audience or travels beyond the business, the quality of your writing affects your career trajectory. Increasing the volume and quality of your output can benefit your career in many ways:

Amplify your efforts: When asked to answer a customer question, you might pick up the phone or send them a quick email. Most people stop there. But successful writers consider packaging the response in a blog post and reaching hundreds or thousands of people who have the same question. Repurposing that blog post into different forms extends your reach further.

Increase your visibility at work: Through writing, you can communicate with people beyond your immediate team. In a larger organization, you won't be the nameless person shuffling past the break room looking for coffee anymore. No, you'll be the person who wrote the thoughtful email or insightful post.

Expand your online presence: No matter how much you love your job, the world is an uncertain place. According to the U.S. Bureau of Labor Statistics, the median length of time in a job is shrinking, down to about 4.2 years. When you change roles, people will search for you online. By writing and publishing in your own name, you can control your appearance to the world at large.

Earn gratitude at work: Modern marketing thrives on employee-generated content. It always needs more. Start contributing blog posts, training materials, or stories, and you may become a hero to your marketing team.

Deepen your expertise: The research, discussion, and thought that goes into writing makes you more of an expert in your field.

> Effective writing clarifies your perspective.

Rethinking Writing in the Workplace

To become more effective, you first have to dispose of a few misconceptions. There's a whole chapter coming up in Part One on workplace myths, but one deserves specific attention: the myth of the Lone Writer.

> In the workplace, no one writes alone.

We *think* that writing is a solitary act, using skills either granted from the heavens or developed during a lengthy career honing the craft. When we envision writers, we picture introverted individuals who would rather navigate the thoughts in their heads than the political and social challenges of the office.

But how well does that model fit the writer in the workplace?

The German novelist and short story writer Franz Kafka worked at an insurance company. I wonder if he wrote a policy compensating the policyholder for turning into a cockroach. Or, imagine being a blog editor talking to William Faulkner: "You really need to break that up into short sentences if you want people to read it online." Individual brilliance does not translate into effectiveness on the job.

No, business writers must collaborate with others to satisfy managers, reviewers, subject matter experts, and specific business audiences.

Successful and valued writes know how to balance two competing sets of skills:

- Navigating the internal processes of writing creatively and productively
- Aligning the content created with business objectives and the work environment

Your inner process depends on the way your particular brain works. It's a fascinating topic, but beyond the scope of this book. (Read more about it in my book *The Writer's Process: Getting Your Brain in Gear.*)

This book deals with the external processes of getting the work done in the work environment. Beyond the writing itself, you encounter challenges such as ambiguous requests, warring decision makers, recalcitrant content experts, unreasonable deadlines, and unending approval processes. In addition, you have to squeeze the focused, contemplative work of writing into your everyday environment, complete with interruptions, distractions, and competing priorities.

Most of us learn these skills on the job, through trial and error. We pay for those trials in time and reputation at work. The experience may diminish our enthusiasm for writing.

There *is* a way to fast-forward that learning process: Discover what works for others and create your own set of writing practices. Adapt, refine, and practice them until you become a valued, successful writer at work.

This book offers processes and practices for being effective and successful on the job.

A Word about Process

In the course of my career, I've worked with well over a hundred technology companies, from established software giants to two-person start-ups. As a freelance writer, I encountered all kinds of situations, including:

- The approver who was a frustrated novelist and wanted to reexamine every word choice
- The subject matter expert who was unwilling to share content
- Clients who kept changing their minds about the objectives during the course of the project
- Content that languished in a never-ending approval process

Each time I encountered one of those obstacles, I came up with a way to avoid it in the future. Eventually I had developed a robust set of processes for writing effective content that met client needs, survived approval processes, and protected my sanity.

These processes, designed to save me trouble, had an unexpected side effect: They improved my client interactions. The work became more collaborative and fun. Following my evolving "standard practices" prevented miscommunication and false starts. It freed my time and energy for creativity, and made the work more fulfilling.

The secret of my writing business essentially boiled down to this: Have a robust process, and you can become a valued contributor.

Everyone benefits from process.

If the workplace tasks come easily to you, or if you have a strong support system at work, remember that the most adept practitioner can be tripped up by unfounded assumptions or miscommunications about purpose. *Process protects the quality of the work.*

Perhaps you're the only writer on your team or work on your own. You do not operate in a vacuum. You need to plan how to reach your audience, and revise to meet their needs. *Process makes you more effective.*

You may excel at crafting beautiful prose, but struggle to navigate the political waters of the business objectives, reviewers, and approvals. *Process protects your time and reputation.*

This book consolidates strategies, checklists, and processes from my own career as well as those of other successful, valued writers. While grammar and sentence construction are critical, you can find those discussions in other books. I'm going to focus on the neglected part of the job of writing: planning and scoping, strategies for collaboration, and risk reduction. This is the stuff they don't teach you in writing class.

How to Use This Book

The book is designed so that you can choose the sections most relevant to your environment, altering and adapting those that best fit your situation.

Part One covers the things typically learned only through hard experience: the myths of writing in the workplace and what the writing job really entails. Because I am an armchair cognitive science geek, it also covers a few psychological concepts that are useful for writers.

Part Two describes project planning, which might be the most important factor in your success as a writer on the job.

Part Three describes the writing process itself; these chapters may help those unproductive writers who struggle to get the work done.

Part Four covers revision. Every great writer is a great reviser.

Part Five is for writers who must navigate external review and approvals. Never get stuck in an endless approval cycle again.

Part Six surveys common problems you may encounter and offers suggestions for getting through them.

The *Resources* section at the end includes checklists and guides that you can adapt for your specific work environment.

With the practices outlined here, you have the tools you need to start doing more writing, with greater success, on the job. Get ready to add *successful, valued writer* to your LinkedIn profile.

Part One: Writing Rules That No One Teaches You

Before you commit to doing more writing at work, get your mindset in order.

Common myths and misconceptions can lead you astray. If you take a narrow view of your responsibilities as a writer, you leave a great deal to chance.

The chapters in this section expand the traditional definition of the writer at work. In addition to assembling words, successful and valued writers practice project management and basic cognitive science. They are team players at work, yet advocate for the reader.

No matter what kind of workplace writer you are today, the lessons of this chapter are key to long-term success.

Chapter 1

Five Myths
That Can Hurt You

Common misconceptions about writers and writing can hurt your chances of success. Let's identify and debunk them here and now.

- The Destiny Myth: Writers are special people
- The Universal Writer Myth: Everyone can write
- The One-Size-Fits-All Myth: Writing is writing
- The Big Idea Myth: The *idea* is the hard part
- The One-Step Writing Myth: Writing is just drafting

The Destiny Myth

Myth: Writing is destiny that people are born to.

Reality: Writing is a skill developed through effort and intention.

Some people imagine that writers are special creatures, sprung from the womb with a thoughtful look and a pen in hand. That's the Destiny Myth, and it quickly becomes a limiting belief.

- If you don't think of yourself as a natural-born writer, you'll avoid jobs or assignments that entail writing. Ultimately, buying into this myth may constrain your career options.
- What if you pride yourself on your prose? If you believe that only "writers" should take on writing tasks, you risk becoming the writer for your group or workplace, pigeonholed into the role. This may limit your career options as well.

It's no myth that writing comes more easily to some people than others. But as the psychologist, professor, and MacArthur genius grant recipient Angela Duckworth points out in her book *Grit*, natural talent is only the starting point for achievement. Effort counts much more. We prefer to attribute success and achievement to talent instead of effort, and that's a problem. Duckworth writes:

> "The 'naturalness bias' is a hidden prejudice against those who've achieved what they have because they worked for it, and a hidden preference for those whom we think arrived at their place because they're naturally talented."

Our persistent belief in talent as the source of success damages both those with natural talent and those who labor diligently for their achievements.

How to counteract the Destiny Myth: If you identify as a writer, let other people know the variety of the tasks involved. Expose the processes. Expose the activities of planning and revising as well as drafting. Encourage others to contribute and write.

The Universal Writer Myth

Myth: Everyone in the workplace should be able to write for the business.

Reality: Not everyone writes *effective* content.

This misconception is almost the opposite of the Destiny Myth, yet it can do as much damage.

The people who promote this belief are often adept with words, exhibiting strong verbal intelligence. They assume that writing is as easy for others as themselves. (People often undervalue their own strengths, not understanding that they are difficult for others.)

The Universal Writer Myth marginalizes the effort involved in effective writing.

Writing *can* be easy if you don't care about who reads your content, or what they think or do after reading it.

In the business context, effective writing is trickier.

> To be a valued writer, you must write valuable content.

Anyone can write 600 words on a topic vaguely related to the job and put it in a blog post. But what does it accomplish?

We've all seen blogs that result from the Universal Writer Myth, populated with content of little value for the prospective audience.

When you write without consideration for the reader, that's called journaling. It's a fine activity for personal development and deep thought, but holds little value beyond yourself.

Writing effectively for business requires that you execute several tasks, including:

- Finding the right tone and style
- Creating content that serves the target audience or advances business objectives
- Fitting the writing work and deadline into existing obligations
- Navigating internal approval and publication processes

How to counteract the Universal Writer Myth: If your workplace adheres to the Universal Writer Myth, the processes described in this book provide critical structure that helps everyone become more effective.

The One-Size-Fits-All Myth

> **Myth**: If you're a good writer, you can write anything with equal ease and success. Writing is writing, right?
>
> **Reality**: Writing has many specialized skill sets; success in one format does not translate automatically to success in others.

Congratulations, you wrote a terrific LinkedIn ad campaign. Since you did so well, why don't you write the product documentation next? This happened to one writer I know at a company she joined. She ran into the One-Size-Fits-All-Myth.

The myth springs from the underlying idea that all writing is alike. Once people find a skilled writer, they ask that person to handle nearly all written communications.

Would you ask the person framing out an industrial warehouse to do detailed finish work on a hand-crafted chair? They might be able to do beautiful woodworking, but you cannot tell by the way that they frame the warehouse. These are different skill sets; success in one does not indicate skill in another.

Writing effective product documentation is a specialized skill. Those who do it well are adept at looking past their existing knowledge and thinking in a linear, logical fashion. Advertising copywriting is a different art form, packing the magic of persuasion into as few words as possible.

Although you may welcome the chance to learn something new, the danger of the One-Size-Fits-All Myth is that others may not realize the learning curve you must tackle. If the people around you believe in this myth, you may be put in a situation in which, working outside your existing competencies, you cannot deliver effective content.

How to counteract the One-Size-Fits-All Myth: Once you start having success as a writer at work, you *will* be asked to take on projects that are outside your comfort zone. You'll have to decide what to do about those requests.

These projects may be wonderful opportunities for growth. If you accept them, let others know that you are building new skills. If asked to write a script for a video when you have not done so before, try responding, "Let me research scriptwriting first, then scope out how much work it will involve." If you're not comfortable or able to invest the time, return with "This is outside my area of expertise. With more time, I could take a class, but we might get better results by hiring a professional scriptwriter."

The Big Idea Myth

Myth: Once you have the big idea, the rest is easy.

Reality: The idea is a starting point; effective execution is most of the work.

Good ideas are everywhere. If ideas were the main factor in writing quality, you could order nearly any book in your favorite genre from Amazon and enjoy it. Hollywood would be filled with terrific movies.

Writers exhibit the Big Idea Myth when they worry about others "stealing their ideas" for the next great blockbuster novel.

> Ideas are abundant. Effective execution is difficult.

The Big Idea Myth is pervasive in the workplace, particularly in businesses with a strong focus on protecting intellectual property.

For writers, the Big Idea Myth can reduce recognition of their effort. Experts deliver dozens of pages of technical content to a writer, who turns it into something wonderful. The expert's name goes on the finished piece, and the writer disappears.

How to counteract the Big Idea Myth. Make the processes described in this book visible to others. Start by collaborating with others during the planning phase, so those around you understand that content must align with a larger plan. Make sure others understand the effort involved in drafting and revising. Demonstrate that execution is critical to success.

The One-Step Writing Myth

Myth: Write the words down and you're done.

Reality: Drafting is the middle of a much longer process.

When you treat the drafting process as the real work of writing, you exhibit the One-Step Writing Myth. This book should dispel that particular myth; writing the first draft is only one small section of the much larger effort.

Writing begins with the planning phase, and it's not done until revision and, ideally, approval and publication. Without planning and research, the writing is difficult. If you stop before the work is out in the world, you cannot be a successful or effective writer.

The One-Step Writing Myth gets you into trouble when used in estimating workload.

For example, imagine that a blog editor asks if you have time to write a 2,000-word post on a topic that you're familiar with. You think, *I can write about 800 words an hour, so I can get this done in three hours with time to spare.* Smiling, you say yes.

Watch out, you've just bought into the One-Step Writing Myth. You forgot about the time to plan the project, to outline, to let the idea simmer in the background, and to revise and polish. You certainly neglected to factor in time for making revisions based on feedback.

Remember that quantity and quality are different measures, each requiring an investment of time. Consider the art of the advertising copywriter, paid large dollar amounts for small numbers of words. The talent is picking the right words.

How to counteract the One-Step Writing Myth: Use the "Scoping and Scheduling the Work" worksheet in the Resources section of this book to include all phases of the process in your planning.

There's one more rampant misconception about writing at work: The Lone Writer Myth. That one gets its own chapter.

Chapter 2

Writing as a Team Sport

As writers, we may think of ourselves as solitary artists, struggling in obscurity. During the drafting phase of writing, most of us do our best work when we are isolated from the distractions of the everyday world. This reality feeds the Lone Writer Myth.

Writers who succeed in the workplace operate effectively in the larger organization. They are *not* solo players. They align their work with the objectives and needs of multiple constituents, including the people paying them to write and the people reading what they produce.

Business writing is a team sport.

Teams vary in size. Your team may be quite large, with:

- Project managers
- Subject matter experts
- Editors
- Proofreaders

- Approvers
- Layout/design staff
- Publication gatekeepers

Perhaps your team is small. Even if you work alone, you owe your position to the *team owners*, the people paying you to do the work in the first place.

To take the sports analogy one step further, every team ultimately serves its fans. For writers, the fans are the readers. If you cannot fill the bleachers with readers, then the work is pointless.

Know Your Position

If you are not finding success in your writing at work, the problem may not lie in your prose. It could be your collaboration skills. If you believe in the Lone Writer Myth, you'll miss the teamwork part of the game, and your work will suffer as a result.

To be a successful and valued writer in the workplace, collaborate with others to set clear objectives, gather research, and create content that serves a larger purpose.

As a writer, you may be the star player on the team. Or, you may operate in the background, a supporting player doing much of the work yet invisible to the fans. This happens when:

- Writing in a corporate or brand voice
- Ghostwriting or blogging for executives
- Collaborating with subject matter experts

I still remember exactly where I was when I learned the truth about press releases: sitting at a desk in an office off

Sand Hill Road in Menlo Park, California, on a sunny spring afternoon. Oak trees swayed outside the window near the desk where I was stationed. As an English major facing an uncertain post-graduation future, I took an internship with a local public relations (PR) firm. PR showed up on the list of careers that English majors should consider.

I was editing a press release and had a problem with the quote attributed to the client's executive. "Then change it," my supervisor said. "We haven't run it by the client yet."

Wait—these quotes aren't verbatim? I never looked at a press release the same way again.

That was the beginning of my ghostwriting experience. I spent most of my career writing in the voice of various brands, corporate executives, subject matter experts, and others.

Disappearing behind others can be difficult if you put your heart and soul into the words. But that is how you serve the work and the reader.

When your name doesn't show up, don't check out of the process. Steer the project until it is out of your hands. Be accountable for its progress. If you take ownership, those around you will understand your role.

The Rules of the Game Change Between Teams

One workplace gives its writers strict processes and templates to follow. Another offers excellent editing, proofreading, and design services. A third (the most common type) leaves the writer with no guidance beyond deadlines.

Writing is a team sport, but when you switch between companies, you might feel that every team plays with a different rule book.

Grammar is the closest thing to a set of rules that you must obey, and even there, adept writers can get creative.

Many businesses observe the Associated Press (AP) style guide or other publications. Those general guides won't help you with planning, scoping, and approval—the "teamwork" part of the writing process. Create your own playbook using the advice and checklists in this book.

Chapter 3

Project Management for Writers

Most books about business writing discuss essential writing skills: sentence construction, grammar, word choice, and style. To thrive in the workplace, you need other skills as well, including:

- Project planning
- Scheduling
- Communicating with content sources and reviewers
- Negotiating conflicting edits or deadline problems

As the writer, you are the product manager for the complete work. The job is more involved than simply putting words into a printed form.

You can craft beautiful sentences, but if they never reach readers, this effort is wasted. You will be a frustrated workplace writer, not a successful one. Take responsibility for the project's overall success by managing it actively.

You Are a Product Manager

Failure to plan can sabotage your writing projects. Common examples of planning failures include:

- Starting the project before clarifying the objectives or identifying stakeholders
- Not allowing sufficient time for revision and review cycles
- Not actively steering work through approvals and reviews

Poor project planning leaves you subject to crisis deadlines, multiple revisions, wasted time, and sour feelings.

An ounce of prevention is worth a pound of revision.

You don't need project management software. In most cases, all you need is a calendar, email or messaging capabilities, and a system for tracking the phases of the project.

This isn't rocket science.

In the Resources section of this book, you will find checklists and a scoping worksheet. Customize them for your organization. The work you do sorting out the planning process can be applied to multiple projects.

In other words, do the work once, and reap the benefits time and again.

Embrace the Project Manager Role

Much of the necessary planning seems like common sense:

- Determine the objective and audience before you write.
- Identify the target tone and style.

- Identify the key stakeholders (people with something at stake in the result).

These directives are so obvious that you might skip right past them, thinking, *I've got this.* You move quickly, relying on your experience and expertise rather than boring process and checklists.

Often, you get by without incident. This success lulls you into a false sense of complacency. Then a project falls apart, and you realize that you failed to identify the stakeholders or craft agreement on the objective.

I want you to be *consistently* successful in your writing. The surest way to get repeatable results is to create a plan and execute it, tracking your progress.

Do you believe that your situation doesn't require project planning? Let's look at the most common reasons for skipping the planning phase.

Everyone already agrees about what's needed.

We tend to hear what we *want* to hear, rather than what the other person actually says. It happens all the time, particularly in the workplace. Cognitive scientists tell us that our *positive confirmation bias* triggers us to look for evidence confirming our viewpoints. We may not sense disagreements or problems until we're in the middle of them.

Take the time to frame the objective and clarify the project, including its deadline. You'll avoid miscommunication.

I'm the only one who needs to sign off on this piece.

When you control publication, you don't have to worry about getting approvals. That's wonderful, but also dangerous. You could end up creating content that is self-indulgent and doesn't meet anyone's needs but your own. Taking the time to identify the objective, the audience, and the reader's reason for caring will make the work more effective, and thus a better use of your time.

We're on a tight deadline—there's no time for planning formalities.

The tighter the schedule, the greater the need for planning. You might condense everything down to a single email that outlines the plan.

"As we talked about in the meeting, I'm writing a blog post about the acquisition, focusing on our investors and customers, to reassure them about our long-term viability. Lee and Joe will approve it. Here are the key points I plan to make: [outline points]. I will send the draft by tomorrow noon, so if you have any objections, say something now."

There. That wasn't so hard. A simple email can prevent a last-minute project from turning into a last-second crisis.

It's a short piece—it doesn't require planning.

Experienced writers may believe they can just "whip something together" and skip over the planning and outlining phase.

I do it myself, and here's what usually happens: I write a quick draft, then decide it's not *quite* right. I tweak a section, and decide to go a different direction. Still not happy, I let it sit a day, then rework it into something else.

Ack! It would have been faster to start with a plan and an outline.

I write when I'm inspired. Planning would get in the way.

Some people only draft when the spirit takes them. Others are still waiting for that spirit. Inspiration is notoriously fickle, and deadlines don't wait.

Worse, we may not feel inspired by our topics until we start writing about them.

If you prefer to draft when inspired, open a file and write whenever the urge strikes. Once you've gotten it out of your system, go back and plan. Revisit the planning checklist in the Resources section. What is the objective? Who is the audience? Why would they read it?

Assess what you have written from this perspective. It might reflect what's going on in *your* head rather than what your audience needs. In that case, edit, rearrange, or retrofit the purpose into what you've written.

Chapter 4

Essential Cognitive Science Concepts

Your job as a writer is to communicate *effectively*. If the prose is beautiful but nobody understands it, then you have failed.

> Without the reader's success, we cannot be effective writers.

Readers are people, and people are complicated. We're not all alike. The way *I* think about a technology may not make sense to you. Information can be lost or misconstrued in the process of traveling from my brain to yours through the written word.

This is where a cognitive science perspective comes in handy. In addition to being a team player and project manager, the successful workplace writer understands the basics of how people think and make decisions. To do that, we turn to cognitive science and behavioral economics.

The Challenges of Business Writing

Because business writing reaches broad and diverse audiences, it is subject to numerous challenges:

Vocabulary and fluency: The reader may not have the same working vocabulary that you do, or share the same native language. When encountering a term, abbreviation, or acronym, the reader might struggle to recall its definition.

Cultural biases and predispositions: The reader may come from a different cultural or professional background, and be unfamiliar with concepts you take for granted. Being alert to cultural biases is particularly important when writing for an international audience. Language is a complex system, and you may not know exactly how it's working in the heads of others.

The reader's current mindset and situation: What will bring readers to your content and how will they encounter it? Are they predisposed to like it or to distrust you? Are they willing to work to decipher concepts that are not clear to them?

Cognitive science gives us useful insights into the challenges of communicating in the business context. In particular, the workplace writer should be familiar with the following concepts:

- Cognitive ease and strain
- The curse of knowledge
- Cognitive empathy

Writing for Cognitive Ease

Behavioral economists and psychologists speak of *cognitive ease* and *cognitive strain*. Cognitive ease is just what it sounds like: the inner sense that things are easy to understand, or that no special, intense mental activity is required. In contrast, a reader experiencing cognitive *strain* must work to understand the material.

Research shows that cognitive ease puts readers in a better mood while making our messages more persuasive.

Run a little test on yourself. The next time you install a software update, read the Terms and Conditions from start to finish, rather than just checking the box claiming you did. If you're an expert in software terms and conditions, find an academic journal article in a field outside your domain. Sit down and read the entire article.

How do you feel now? Happy? Relaxed? Probably not.

For most of us, reading legal contracts and academic journal articles is an exercise in cognitive strain. Our brains strain to make sense of the text. Often, we bail out and just check the box.

Let's not make readers face that same decision to either power through or leave.

Everything from font selection and layout to word choice affects cognitive ease.

In the book *Thinking, Fast and Slow*, Daniel Kahneman describes research that asked people to evaluate identical reports from one of two fictitious firms: one had an easy-to-pronounce name, and the other was more difficult. Respondents weighted the advice from the first firm more highly.

Kahneman suggests: "If you quote a source, choose one with a name that is easy to pronounce."

If we all agree on the importance of writing for the reader's fluidity, the question remains: Why is it so difficult to write this way?

Because it's hard to get out of your own head. That's the curse of knowledge.

The Curse of Knowledge

What happens when you combine technology geeks and healthcare professionals? You get a perfect storm of buzzwords.

This is the headline of an IBM press release from December 20, 2016, announcing a collaboration with the Cleveland Clinic: "Cleveland Clinic, IBM Continue Their Collaboration to Establish Model for Cognitive Population Health Management and Data-Driven Personalized Healthcare."

I'm with them as far as the part about the continued collaboration. When I encounter "establish model" I start wondering what exactly they are announcing. By the time I reach "cognitive population health management," I start wondering what's in my Netflix queue.

The title clearly makes sense to the person (or people) who wrote it. But it's a press release intended for the general media, investors, and others. So why can't I make sense of it?

Let's be clear: I'm not picking on IBM or public relations professionals. Every industry has its share of buzzwords and jargon. Industry terminology streamlines communications by serving as a shortcut for complicated topics. But when used outside the appropriate context, terminology becomes jargon, plaguing marketing, sales, and public relations efforts.

Why do well-meaning people put this stuff out into the world?

Because once you know something, it's difficult to "unknow" it.

Behavioral economists call this the *curse of knowledge*. It's the difficulty of imagining that other people don't know what we know.

We have all experienced it, both as victim and perpetrator. You've seen it in action throughout your life: the physician who delivers a diagnosis peppered with medical terms, or the auto mechanic explaining details of the compression engine to a confused customer. College students suffer from it when a professor overestimates the students' background and delivers a lecture that no one can understand.

In his book *The Sense of Style: The Thinking Person's Guide to Writing in the 21ˢᵗ Century*, Harvard psychologist Steven Pinker writes, "The curse of knowledge is the single best explanation I know of why good people write bad prose. It simply doesn't occur to the writer that her readers don't know what she knows."

This curse affects academicians, technical experts, lawyers, and financial professionals, or anyone immersed in a field of study, fluent with its terminology and abstract concepts.

> The greater your knowledge, the stronger the curse of knowledge.

To write effectively, you'll need to defeat this ingrained mental tendency. Take your reader's perspective and try to imagine what they know. Consult other people in similar roles. When using terminology, ask yourself whether it is right for the audience.

To avoid the curse of knowledge, seek to understand the reader's *cognitive* state. To write effective copy, understand their *emotional* state. For that, you need cognitive empathy.

Cognitive Empathy

To figure out why a reader might bother to read and act on what you write, understand what motivates them and their current mindset.

Psychologists distinguish between different types of empathy: emotional, cognitive, and compassionate. Effective writers develop *cognitive empathy*, or the intentional effort to understand what another person is thinking or feeling, taking their perspective.

To develop cognitive empathy, try to put yourself in the reader's situation and understand their mindset. What does the reader bring to the piece you're writing?

For example, will the reader be a prospective customer exploring solutions? If so, what kinds of problems are they trying to solve? What's at stake? Try to establish a relationship or earn trust before diving in with a sales pitch.

Are you writing content for a support forum that customers visit when they have problems? If so, the reader might be frustrated or feeling stressed when they find your content.

When under stress, we tend to make decisions quickly, often without rational analysis. If your reader will approach the work feeling stressed, don't lead with a lengthy discussion about data. The emotional parts of their brains take over under stress; consider leading with a story or an acknowledgment of the problem. Package any data or facts for easy and fast consumption.

When you intentionally try to understand the emotional state of the target audience, you exercise cognitive empathy. You don't have to *feel* the customer's emotions, but you can imagine them and take their perspective. This will make your writing more effective.

Chapter 5

You Are
The Reader's Advocate

In addition to being a project manager, cognitive scientist, and team player, the successful business writer fills yet another role: *reader's advocate.*

Effective content meets the needs of the audience. This is true whether you're writing for partners, investors, or colleagues and management within your organization. Effective writing meets their needs, and you're the one who must stand up for them.

Learn how to fill the role of reader's advocate with grace.

The Challenges of Representing the Reader

Being the reader's advocate may put you in an awkward position. You have to ask questions like "Who cares about this new feature?" or "Why would someone want to read about our CEO?"

When you get into the reader's mindset, you can see the weaknesses in your current objectives. You may be the first person to point out flaws in the party line.

If this happens, stand up for the reader without introducing conflict.

Sometimes you can do this effectively through the act of writing. (*Use your words*, as parents often say.)

For example, if the user interface is awkward to use, write up a detailed description of how it works from an outsider's perspective. Pass that draft around for an early review to those involved in designing the user interface. This helps the people involved see past their own perspectives and biases.

> Writing shows us the world through others' eyes. Be the guide.

The Benefits of Taking the Reader's Viewpoint

Speaking up on behalf of the audience increases your value to your employer. If you become known as someone who takes the customer's perspective, others may seek your input on their projects.

If you work in a culture that's unwilling to consider outside perspectives or look beyond its own way of thinking—well, perhaps it's time to use the strategies in this book to tune your writing skills and find a different position. Once you've learned how to be valued and successful as a writer in the workplace, you can take those skills to other jobs. You might need to do so anyway. A business that insulates itself from the opinions of those it serves isn't likely to last.

Chapter 6

Process Is
Your Secret Weapon

The chapters in this section have presented the challenges facing the writer on the job: pervasive misconceptions about writing, the need to collaborate and work on a team while taking ownership of the project, cognitive biases, and advocating for the reader.

If you're like many of us, you navigate these hurdles in an ad hoc way each time you take on a project, with varying degrees of success. You win some, you lose some, right?

You will get better, more predictable results by creating and adhering to a process.

While process may sound like unnecessary work added to the task of writing, it's the best path to consistent success and productive output. The small up-front investment in establishing your process pays off, again and again, with every project you do.

Process protects us from impatience, misunderstandings, and political undercurrents. A skilled writer without a strong process will have mixed success in the workplace.

> To become a valued writer, own your process.

The Power of Process

In my career consulting with technology companies, clients occasionally called me in as a *fixer*. They needed an outsider to salvage an important project that stalled out or was unable to get through approvals. Some of these troubled papers and reports had been through so many revision cycles and editors that they became strange, Franken-documents that nobody could love or agree on.

Microsoft Word has a "change tracking" feature that lets reviewers leave their comments and edits in the document for others to approve. The markups spoke volumes about what had happened during the revision process. Outright arguments sometimes erupted in the comments in the margins.

Those edits were symptoms of miscommunication and poor planning. Instead of fixing the document, I repaired the process.

Inevitably, I would put aside the heavily marked-up draft and restart the project from the beginning, creating a version that satisfied everyone. Was this success due to the brilliance of my writing?

Not really.

As a consultant, I brought along my own processes for articulating the project needs, structuring the solution, and paving the way for approvals. From analyzing the corpse of the previous version of the document, I already knew the potential disagreements and could address them ahead of time. My real value in those situations was not my writing skill; it was my ability to identify and meet the client's objectives and audience needs.

Ah, the magic of process. It can make you seem brilliant.

Experienced writers and creative individuals may resist the idea of adhering to a defined set of steps for planning and approvals. The pushback sounds like this:

I don't need to use a list—I have great instincts.

I've been getting along fine so far...

Experienced writers don't follow the same process all the time.

You *could* trust in your own instinct and hope not to miss anything. Or, you could take a page from pilots, construction management projects, and surgical teams, and protect yourself from failure by following a simple plan.

Checklists

Gazing idly out the window as we descended into Hartford-Springfield airport, I watched the buildings and cars grow larger and closer. My husband, Steve, and I had flown to Hartford many times to visit family, and this flight seemed like all the others. Suddenly, the plane suddenly accelerated, gained altitude, and executed a wide loop to approach the airport again.

Steve pointed out that he heard the landing gear dropping during the *second* approach, but didn't recall hearing it the first time. I'm no pilot, but it seems that it's much better to land with the wheels down than up.

We could only guess that the landing process was under way when somebody realized that the wheels were not lowered. It's quite possible that those of us on that flight owe our lives to a landing checklist.

The airline industry relies heavily on checklists to ensure passenger safety. In *The Checklist Manifesto,* the writer, surgeon and public health researcher Atul Gawande describes the use of checklists in aviation and other fields. He makes a compelling case for using checklists in any high-stakes situation in which complexity and unexpected problems can be deadly.

A simple checklist serves two important purposes:

1. The checklist protects us from oversights and human fallibility: the *one* time someone forgets a critical task or assumes that someone else has already done it.

2. Running through a checklist creates an opportunity for team communication. The act of talking through the items and describing plans gets everyone working toward a common goal, and ensures that specialists look beyond their own domains.

Gawande writes, "Checklists seem to be able to defend anyone, even the experienced, against failure in many more tasks than we realized. They provide a kind of cognitive net. They catch mental flaws inherent in all of us—flaws of memory and attention and thoroughness."

In writing, the risks are obviously less perilous than those facing the surgeon or pilot. Usually, no one dies if you mangle a sentence or write a boring report. But you are committing time that could be spent doing other things. You may also be staking your personal or professional reputation on the result.

A checklist is the physical manifestation of a basic process, and it supports both individual and team endeavors.

When it comes to critical work, the most skilled practitioners know that finding and adhering to a proven process keeps them out of trouble. Wouldn't you like those same assurances in your job?

The Elements of the Workplace Writer's Process

I don't believe in process for its own sake. Bureaucracy and unnecessary procedures quickly become barriers to creativity and productivity. No one likes stultifying process.

As with aviation checklists, the value comes from identifying the *critical points* in the project at which you should stop and confirm that you have taken the steps that protect you from failure. These checklists should be short, outlining the most important steps. In writing, simple checklists might include the following:

Before writing: Know who the key decision makers are. Make sure everyone is in agreement on objectives for the piece and the target audience. If you anticipate a contentious review, plan the approval process.

When ready to write: Plan how to do the work in the time allotted. Decide how you will approach the draft (an outline).

During revision: Confirm that the content meets the project objectives. Run spelling and grammar checks. Search for terminology or acronyms that may confuse the target audience.

Before reviews and approvals: Identify the reviewers and approvers. Communicate clearly your expectations from the review. Schedule time to integrate the comments.

The Resources section includes sample checklists; visit AnneJanzer.com/WWP to download templates you can customize yourself.

The chapters that follow offer guidelines and suggestions for each of these phases. I believe that these simple practices are the best way to ensure consistent, successful results. They are the secret sauce to my writing career. Use these ingredients to develop your own recipe for success.

Part Two: The Planning Process

It's *so* tempting to jump in and start writing when you have a new project. Yet in most cases, you'll get better results in less time when you stop and make a plan first. A few minutes of advance planning can save hours of work and frustration during revision and review cycles.

Creating and sharing a plan protects you from miscommunication. It is much easier to change course *before* you start writing rather than during reviews, when you have invested work in creating the draft and the deadline looms.

Careful planning also accelerates the review and approval process because it divides discussions about the project into two distinct phases:

1. *What* you want to do (discussed before drafting)

2. *How* you executed those objectives (discussed during reviews)

Use the guidance in this section for the first set of discussions, forging agreements on direction and objectives before you write.

Remember the types of workplace writers from the introduction? If you're an inadvertent writer today, use the practices in this chapter to focus on the work in an intentional way. If you're overburdened or frustrated, address your problems through careful planning.

Chapter 7

The Planning Overview

If writing is a team sport, then the planning process is the pre-game strategy session. This is when you nail down positions and game plan.

Every project benefits from this effort, although the results will differ in depth and detail. This chapter outlines three variations on the project plan:

- Choose the *minimum viable plan* for straightforward projects or when you're operating on your own.
- The *complete plan* prevents miscommunication when working on a team or on complex projects with many contributors or stakeholders.
- Pull out the *bulletproof plan* when you sense that the project could run into trouble in the review process, if the topic is sensitive, or when the deadline is tight.

The Minimum Viable Plan

Assemble a minimum plan by deciding the following six points:

1. **The objective**: What do you hope to accomplish with this piece?

2. **The audience**: Who is the target reader?

3. **The reader's reason**: Why is someone going to read this? What would they hope to get from it?

4. **The format**: How will people find and interact with this content? Will readers be using mobile phones? Should it be a lengthy paper or a short blog post?

5. **The review process**: Who needs to sign off on the piece? Who will offer feedback?

6. **The schedule**: When will you deliver the first draft, and how much time will you allow for revisions?

Write down your thoughts about each phase. If you are working on a team or within a group, share these points with others before you start, to surface any unspoken assumptions or potential disagreements up front.

This communication might be quite simple:

"I'm writing a blog post targeting the technical decision maker in the pharmaceutical industry, encouraging them to register for our webinar. The post will describe how our software solves problems when collaborating across national boundaries. I'll send you the first draft by Tuesday the 12th. That should give us time for reviews and revisions on Wednesday so it can go live on Thursday the 14th."

This email is enough to share the plan with people on your team.

The Complete Plan

Once you agree on what a successful outcome looks like, you can then work backward and write exactly that piece. That's the idea behind the complete plan.

The complete plan is a more detailed version of the minimum plan. Use it to gain approval from key participants before you begin drafting.

In particular, add detail to point 5, the review process, by answering the following questions:

- Who are the people affected by this project—the key stakeholders?
- Whose approval will you need?
- Who else should review or comment on the draft?

Note that reviewers and approvers hold different roles.

Reviewers get a chance to read and comment on the piece. Depending on their authority and expertise, you may not need to act on those comments. For example, a writer or editor may retain editorial control over tone and style. Subject matter experts weigh in on factual content, and legal teams on issues of liability. Although you may welcome comments outside the reviewer's defined area, you can choose whether or not to implement them. You might disregard the legal team's comment on a stylistic nuance in the piece.

The **approvers** either actively sign off or have the chance to veto a project before publication.

When you identify the key players before you start writing, you can take their perspectives into consideration or run ideas by them in advance, for an easier approval process.

The Bulletproof Plan

The person asking you to write a project doesn't meet your eyes while speaking with you. You have heard that a colleague has already tried to do the project and put it aside, or it lingered mysteriously untouched. Perhaps you sense in your stomach that you're about to undertake a high-risk endeavor.

Time to pull out the bulletproof plan.

OK, it's not really bulletproof, or fail-safe, or any of those superlatives. However, executing this plan increases your odds of success on projects that are at risk of failure. When you succeed with high-profile and challenging assignments, you earn recognition from others who know what's going on. You move one step closer to being a "successful and valued" writer at work.

To create a bulletproof plan, start by assembling the complete plan, then add the following two steps:

1. Decide questions of authority ahead of time
2. Get pre-approval on the objectives and outline before writing

Decide Questions of Authority in Advance

You've sent a detailed blog post about a new product initiative out for external review. You think you've done a terrific job of explaining it, complete with a clever baseball metaphor.

The developer thinks the metaphor is a perfect fit. The Chief Technology Officer (CTO) suggests using a metaphor involving his favorite pastime, yacht racing.

Whose opinion should you act on?

a) The person with the most knowledge of the technology (the developer)

b) The person who is highest on the organization chart (the CTO)

c) You, the author

That's why you decide issues of authority in advance.

(The right answer in this situation is the person representing the reader: *you*. If the metaphor is technically accurate, try testing it with someone from the target audience.)

Before the people have a chance to review the work, decide who has the final authority on issues of style, technical content, legal or regulatory issues, brand positioning, and so on.

If you wait until the review process to ask these questions, the debate can become personal. Lay them out in advance, and everyone can agree based on abstract reason rather than personal preference. If and when conflicts arise, you'll have a guideline for handling them.

The bulletproof plan describes these levels of authority clearly and explicitly. For example:

- The legal or compliance team can review any claims made in the document.

- The marketing team should act as advocates for the target readers.

- The technical team is responsible for confirming accuracy of the content.
- The C-suite can override the decision to publish.
- The editor has final say on tone and style.

Solicit Approval Before Writing

The secret to the bulletproof plan is getting an explicit go-ahead from the approvers and key reviewers *before* you start. This sign-off is what makes the plan bulletproof (or as close to it as you can get).

Frame this extra approval cycle as an outline review.

Don't share a detailed, working outline; reviewers might start discussing word choice. Provide the general flow or key points that you plan to communicate. That should be enough for most people.

At the top of the outline, list the key planning decisions that you've made:

- Objective
- Target audience
- Reader's reason for reading (and any call to action)
- Format, including tone and style
- Review process, identifying reviewers and approvers
- Schedule

Then add the quick outline or list of key points and send it around for approval. Anyone who signs off on the outline is also agreeing with the planning decisions

Taking this step clarifies any assumptions that you or others may be making. It prevents you from going down the wrong path, writing content that needs extensive reworking or will never gain approval.

Pre-approval also streamlines the review process. When it comes to the review, invite people to comment on *how the piece executes* those core objectives, which were already approved.

The rest of the chapters in this section cover six key elements of the project plan: objective, audience, reader's reason, format, review plan, and schedule.

Chapter 8

Why Are You Writing?

Here's a hypothetical scenario:

Marketing: "We need a blog post about the new feature. Can you write one?"

You: "Okay, I'll get you a post by Friday."

You write a detailed technical post about the feature, highlighting the performance challenges your team has overcome and the excellence of the overall design.

Then you discover that marketing manager who asked for the post wanted to entice existing customers to try the feature by discussing how it addresses urgent business problems.

Those differences only surface during the review and approval process. After several back-and-forth passes, you publish an awkward, heavily revised post that attempts to please everyone but that bores the reader.

This happens when you start writing without stopping to ask why.

You cannot be effective without an objective.

Whether you plan to write a blog post, contributed article, technical paper, website copy, investor report, or email to the management team, don't start without a goal in mind.

Unless that objective is explicit, the possibilities for miscommunication are huge. In the example above, the marketing manager *assumed* that you knew what they needed. You assumed that you understood what type of post people wanted to read. We each filter what we hear through our own expectations.

Objectives, Big and Small

Most business content serves at least *two* sets of objectives. Think of them as a *macro* objective and a *micro* objective.

The macro objective serves the purpose of the person or group commissioning the piece. The micro objective addresses the reader, and is typically the responsibility of the writer to discover. It describes the specific purpose of the piece: who is reading this, and what they should do as a result.

For example, a blog post might have the following macro and micro objectives:

Macro: Demonstrate *thought leadership* in our industry

Micro: Make the customers feel like they've made a great decision, and get prospects to sign up for a related webinar

The goals for a lead generation paper might look like this:

Macro: Move prospects through the sales cycle

Micro: Address the specific concerns of the compliance teams at prospects' companies.

An internal project-planning document has objectives as well:

Macro: Request resources from management and clarify the project

Micro: Get people excited about working on this project

A tightly prescribed regulatory filing might meet goals such as:

Macro: Satisfy the regulator's requirements

Micro: Demonstrate to investors who see the document that your organization has top talent working on this project

Try this yourself with the business communications you encounter. If you get an email from a company, the micro objective should be easy to spot. It's the reason they sent *you* the email. See if you can also detect the bigger picture goal. Are they trying to earn your trust or loyalty? Sell you more stuff?

Think about what it feels like to receive these communications before you start writing them.

The worst thing you can do is to start writing without any clear objective. The next-worst thing is to start writing with only a vague objective, such as:

- Feed the blog
- Generate leads
- Nurture leads
- Communicate with customers

These high-level goals are not enough to create effective content. Before you set out to write anything, decide on the detailed, micro purpose. That insight will shape how you structure and write the piece. To find the micro objective, you'll need to know the target audience.

Chapter 9

Who Will Read It?

We live inside our own heads. It's tempting to imagine that everyone else is in there with us, viewing the world the way we do.

They aren't. And they don't.

You can, however, use the planning phase to temporarily inhabit the minds of your target audience.

The General Audience

The target audience is the core of every objective.

Your big-picture, macro objective offers the first clue into the general audience you want to reach. Possible candidates include:

Existing customers

Prospective customers

A specific segment of prospective customers

Industry analysts

Investors

Prospective employees

Government regulators

Partners

One piece of content frequently serves multiple audiences. For example:

- The industry analyst might read a blog post reaching out to a customer and be intrigued to learn more.
- Existing customers see marketing materials targeting prospects and feel better (or worse) about their purchases.
- Potential employees read web pages or blog posts and form opinions about the company.
- Investors follow the blog and press releases for reassurance that you're not burning through all that cash playing Ping-Pong and drinking beer.

Although secondary audiences are valuable and important, effective writing develops from having a clear primary audience. Choose one and execute well, and everything else is a bonus.

The audience can be quite specific: I once wrote a lengthy, detailed paper for a start-up to satisfy exactly one corporate prospect. My client was just getting started, and landing this customer would be a huge deal. The target audience was a small technical team at a single company—maybe half a dozen people.

After signing that customer, the company continued send the paper to other prospects who needed similar technical detail. Those additional audiences were a fortunate by-product of the process. The initial piece was effective because it met the needs of a precise, targeted audience.

The Audience Avatar

When thinking about audience needs, focus on readers as *people*, rather than roles and demographics.

Once you've identified the target audience, come up with a mental image of the reader. The more specific you can be, the better. Summon an image of a real person, if possible.

Your marketing organization may have buyer personas like Ted the Sys Admin and Jill the CFO. These personas can be useful when writing for customers. However, you may want to reach investors, prospective employees, partners, regulators, executive teams, and others. Marketing personas won't take you there.

Rather than go through a lengthy persona-development exercise for each role, rummage around in your memory for people who fit those roles. Find a person from your past or present who serves as a reasonable substitute or prototype for the target audience.

- That guy in finance who does absolutely everything in spreadsheets might be a prime example of a critical reader for the financial audience.
- Your sister-in-law, who reads the *Harvard Business Journal* religiously, would be a good person to target with this "thought leadership" piece.

Let's call this person your *audience avatar.*

If you don't know anyone in the role, that's OK. Think of a colleague, friend, or family member. You'll get the best results when imagining a person who has the following attributes:

- This person may not have your depth of expertise in the subject, nor would you expect them to.
- You like and respect the person: a sense of affection makes your tone and style comfortable to read.

One woman I know transformed her writing from an impersonal "human resources" style to personable and inviting by envisioning her teenage daughter as she wrote. Her daughter was intelligent, but knew nothing about the business arena. Because this woman loves her daughter, her writing style became warm and friendly.

Using an adolescent as an avatar has a secondary benefit: Teenagers are quick to detect condescension. Imagining the eye roll will prevent you from oversimplifying or talking down to the audience.

Chapter 10

Why Should They Care?

For centuries, philosophers have debated the question: If a tree falls in a forest and no one hears it, does it make a sound?

Here's an update that's relevant to today's business world: If nobody reads your "thought leadership" content, is it thought leadership?

For your content to be effective, your target audience has to consume it (reading, viewing, or listening). Readers need motivation to spend their time and attention. Give them a reason.

If you're following the six steps of the project plan, by now you have identified the business objective for this project. You may know the macro and micro goals.

If you're focused on your own reasons alone, then the writing will seem self-serving.

Look for the purpose beyond yourself: the *reader's reason*. Consider how this content serves the reader. Will it:

- Entertain?
- Educate?
- Solve a specific problem?
- Make them feel better about themselves?
- Inspire them?
- Fill a regulatory requirement?

It's *never* really about you. Documents like annual reports, which are ostensibly all about the company, fill the needs of investors, regulators, prospects, and others.

Summon the reader avatar, put yourself in their place (using cognitive empathy), and ask yourself why you should care. Why would you bother to click through from a headline, download the content, or read past the first paragraph?

> Every piece of content should offer value to the reader.

In one consulting engagement, I worked with an engineering team to document the architecture of the current product. That technical document had a well-defined target audience: the developers. The reader's reasons were also clear.

1. New hires could read the document to get up to speed quickly, figuring out how everything fit together.

2. Developers could reference the document when they had to cover one another's absences.

Keeping those objectives in mind helped me make decisions about format, structure the document, and write something that served the business.

If you do not know why the audience would want to read what you're writing, rethink what you're doing.

Once you have identified the reader's reason, the writing path becomes clearer. That motivation guides your choices in planning and drafting alike.

Chapter 11

What Will It Look Like?

"Form follows function" is a well-known saying in architecture and design. It applies to writing as well. Decisions about format flow from choices about the objective, audience, and reader's reasons.

Businesses may choose a particular form because other companies in their industry use it and they want to adhere to standard practices. Doing what everyone else does may feel like the safest choice.

Human beings have a powerful urge to conform to social norms. Even renegade founders, bent on disrupting industries, look around to see what other start-ups are doing or seek advice about best practices from investors. Several start-up executives have said to me, "We've been told that we should have three white papers and a data sheet at launch time, so let's do them."

White papers aren't *always* the first thing you should do, nor the best way to meet your objectives. The urge to conform can interfere with serving the reader.

Consider the possible advantage you could gain reaching your audience in a fresh and effective way.

What are your objectives? How does your target audience prefer to receive the information you're providing? The written word may not be the right choice. Perhaps you should create a video, infographic, or a recorded whiteboard talk instead. If you plan to write, consider how you might adapt the content to different forms.

Decide before you write.

The Form Informs the Writing

Having a form imposes constraints on the writing, and constraints can be our friends.

In *The Myths of Creativity*, author and business school professor David Burkus defines the Constraints Myth as the belief that creativity flourishes only when you can work without limits on your time, resources, or output. We use this myth to blame external events for a lack of creativity, or as an excuse to wait for the perfect alignment of time and space before we act.

If the Constraints Myth were true, why would poets write sonnets? In fact, how would anything be created at all? Very few people have unlimited time and resources to respond to creative impulses and carry them through to completion. Everyone works under constraints.

With strict limits, your brain works harder to make connections and fit the content to the form. That mental work spurs creativity and originality.

Knowing the form in advance also affects the tone and style of the words you create.

When writing a book, you can construct long sentences with multiple clauses, like this one. But what if you're writing text that people will read online, or on a mobile phone, with a small screen?

Use short sentences and paragraphs.

Avoid multiple clauses in a single sentence.

Knowing the final form guides you in creating an appropriate first draft.

Scope the Details

Having chosen the final form, consider the details.

- How long should the final product be? Are your readers likely to take the time to read a four-page paper? A ten-page document?
- Does it need graphics? Charts? Screen images or videos?
- Will people read from beginning to end or skim through looking for specific content?
- What is the appropriate tone and style?
- If you have a great deal of content to convey, should you break it into a series? Compile it into an ebook?

Start with a general plan, but keep your options open. You may change course based on what you discover during writing.

Plan for the Future

Nearly anything you write can be repurposed in other formats. Thinking about those possibilities at the outset makes future reworking easier.

As a bonus, distributing content across multiple formats makes it accessible to a wider audience. For example, as you write a technical white paper, identify areas or subtopics that would make effective blog posts. Create posts pointing people to the white paper. That's a win–win: meaty blog content *and* additional traffic to the paper.

Length Matters

You may have heard it a thousand times before, but the right answer to "How long should this be?" is always "As long as it needs to be." You might start writing something long and run out of steam, or get going on a blog post and realize you've got a series. Be flexible.

Remember, though, that readers have expectations.

Understand the standards for the format you are working with. If a prospective customer gives you their email address in exchange for a nicely designed ebook, they expect more than two pages of content. Many magazines and online blogs provide suggested word counts for the articles and posts they publish.

Writers who understand the expectations of a specific form can break those rules effectively.

Marc Andreessen, a venture capitalist at Andreessen Horowitz, used to publish diatribes on Twitter by combining them in sequentially numbered posts, in a "tweetstorm." He took a form with well-understood limitations (140-character limit) and created a plan to regularly work beyond those limits.

With general agreement on the length and format of a piece, you are ready to create a tentative schedule for the work.

Chapter 12

When Will It Be Done?

Successful scheduling is part guesswork, part math, and part luck, with a little self-knowledge thrown into the mix.

Each project and work environment has its own variations. You may have a firm publication deadline and a date by which you'll receive necessary content. The rest is up to you. With intentional practice, you can learn to create schedules that work.

This chapter covers strategies for accurate scheduling, starting with self-knowledge.

Scheduler, Know Thyself

Daniel Kahneman and Amos Tversky coined the term *planning fallacy* to refer to the unfounded optimism that leads us to underestimate potential problems. According to Kahneman, we focus on what we already know. (In this case, our plans.) We are cognitively lazy about seeking out examples that contradict what we want to believe. This innate bias leads us to underemphasize potential problems.

As Kahneman writes in *Thinking, Fast and Slow*, "The successful execution of a plan is specific and easy to imagine when one tries to forecast the outcome of a project. In contrast, the alternative of failure is diffuse, because there are immeasurable ways for things to go wrong."

Envisioning success is fun. *Counting* on easy success gets us in trouble when unanticipated problems arise, as they frequently do. If you plan to finish a project the day you publish it, then a malfunctioning computer or late approval can throw off the schedule. The best schedules include contingency plans and leave room for the unexpected.

There's another cognitive concept that you should consider when planning: *the incubation effect*. Whether or not you've heard the term, I guarantee that you've experienced the incubation effect in your life. It's what happens when you leave the office after struggling with a topic, only to come up with a solution later that night or early the next morning.

Background processes in your brain keep working on unfinished tasks while you're not paying attention. You are incubating ideas like a hen incubating her eggs, but without always being aware of it.

Incubation is an essential part of the creative process. In his book *Creativity: Flow and the Psychology of Discovery and Invention*, psychologist Mihaly Csikszentmihalyi reports that significant creative breakthroughs happen after a period of struggle followed by rest and pondering. The background processes of the brain need time to make connections.

Incubation increases your writing productivity by enlisting mental cycles during nonworking times, such as sleeping, eating, showering, commuting, and exercising. To reap these benefits, leave time in the schedule for incubation, fitting slices of downtime into your plans.

Scoping and Scheduling:
Calendar Time vs. Effort Time

When planning the execution of a project, you work with two distinct variables:

Calendar time: How much time will elapse on the calendar (or clock, for a short project) from start to finish?

Effort time: How much time are you spending on this project that could be spent on other activities?

Figuring out this variable is usually referred to as *scoping*.

Project schedules usually deal in calendar time because people care about *when* a job can be finished. To create realistic schedules, or to accept or reject a project, you must first do the scoping, determining how much *effort* it will require.

Effort time should not equal calendar time.

If you have only an hour, then that's all the effort you can possibly invest in the project. In general, don't compress the calendar time to match the effort time you plan to spend. Despite the apparent logical appeal, our brains don't work well this way.

Always leave time in the schedule for planning and incubation.

Even if you love operating under a looming deadline, writing work usually suffers under extreme time pressure. You may shortcut revision and editing, or bypass proofreading.

The counterintuitive truth is that you invest *less* effort by allowing enough calendar time but using it wisely, because of the incubation effect. With sufficient elapsed time, your brain can work when you are not paying attention, shrinking the intentional effort you invest in the project.

Reverse-Engineer the Schedule

The best way to schedule is to plan backward from the final deadline, allotting time available for the essential phases of the work:

- Writing, including research and interviews, outlining, and drafting
- Revision
- External reviews and approvals (if necessary)

If you don't have a final deadline, create one based on reasonable estimates and sufficient incubation time. Deadlines provide the necessary urgency to get the work done.

The writing schedule varies depending on your writing and revision practices. Try tracking your projects until you get a sense of your pace. You'll come to understand how long you spend in each phase and what sort of break you prefer during working sessions. Some people can write for hours on end. Most of us tire after an hour or ninety minutes and need a break.

For a short project like a blog post, you may be able to research, outline, and draft in a single working session. If possible, build in an overnight break before revising and proof-reading so that you can see the work with fresh eyes.

Longer projects may require lengthier research phases and multiple drafting sessions. Learn what works for you and include it in your plans and schedules.

Avoid Common Planning Mistakes

Schedules typically diverge from reality because people make one of the following common planning errors.

Delaying the start. When you have plenty of time, it's tempting to delay starting until the deadline approaches. If possible, don't wait to immerse yourself in the topic.

By starting early, you put the incubation effect to work. Also, when you start researching and outlining, you may discover unexpected avenues to explore or potential pitfalls.

Scheduling based on word count. *This brief should be about 1,000 words. I can write 500 words an hour, so two hours is a good estimate.*

Word count is a lousy metric for the amount of time required for a project, for two reasons.

1. It ignores the non-drafting parts of the process, including research, outlining, and revision.
2. Effort doesn't correlate directly with word count. To paraphrase the famous mathematician and physicist Blaise Pascal, "If I'd had more time, I would have written a shorter letter." Shorter can be harder. Ask any marketing copywriter.

Each written piece consumes a baseline level of effort, no matter how many words it includes. Account for that baseline in your estimates.

Not leaving enough time for revision. Revision is when *blah* writing becomes interesting or compelling. When schedules are tight, revision slides off the plate.

> If you don't schedule for revision, you are planning for mediocrity.

Giving reviewers and approvers too much time. Just like writers, reviewers will delay reading until the last possible moment. Whether you give a reviewer a day, a week, or a month to comment on your project, the effort they expend is the same. A shorter deadline imparts urgency. A week is almost always enough, and probably too long in most situations. (See Part Five: The Review Process, for more guidance.)

Best-case-scenario planning. Have you seen the series of *Worst-Case Scenario Survival* books by David Borgenicht, Joshua Piven and other authors? These books offer advice on what to do in incredibly unlikely situations. The work-related book tells you how to survive if you are trapped in an office supply closet.

Too often, we make plans that are similarly far-fetched in hindsight, based on *best-case* scenarios. We schedule assuming that everything will go perfectly.

- No key person will get sick.
- No project will be delayed.
- No one will have a computer malfunction.
- Everything will be wonderful.

We live in an imperfect world. Between the planning fallacy and the unpredictable nature of the workplace, things usually take longer than we think they will. Add a buffer to the schedule.

I spent many years working as a freelance writer. Before each project, I'd make an estimate of the effort time involved, adding a 20 percent buffer for emergencies. Then I tracked the work and compared it to my estimates. I used the "emergency" buffer on nearly half of the projects. I'm an eternal optimist.

When the unexpected happens, you'll be glad you added a buffer. If everything goes smoothly, you'll look efficient.

> People don't get upset if you deliver work ahead of schedule.

Handling Time Crunches

When calendar time is short, plan carefully to fit the effort time required into the available days.

If possible, don't steal time from either planning or writing phases.

To fit the work into a limited amount of calendar time, try:

- Starting as early as possible
- Compressing (but not eliminating) incubation time, taking advantage of overnight stops in multi-day projects
- Enlisting other people to work on editing and revision, freeing yourself to focus on drafting

- Getting commitments from reviewers to turn around revisions quickly

Adding people rarely works for the drafting phase of projects, although you can request outside help for revision and proofreading.

Perhaps the best thing you can do is clear the deck for the writing. Reduce distractions and interruptions, cancel meetings, and work whenever and wherever you focus best.

Part Three: The Drafting Process

With a plan in hand, you're ready to start the work of writing.

Don't fall prey to the One-Step Writing Myth. Account for all the phases of writing, including:

- Research
- Outlining
- Drafting
- Layering

When you break the work into its component phases, you bring the right mindset and physical environment to each stage. Schedule incubation time between the steps for streamlined effort and better results.

The chapters in this section offer advice for getting through the drafting phase as efficiently and pleasantly as possible.

If you sometimes identify as an unproductive writer, use the steps described here to divide the work and power through it efficiently. If you are a reluctant or inadvertent writer, breaking the work into its component parts makes it easier to accomplish.

Chapter 13

The Ins and Outs of Research

Some projects entail a great deal of research: interviewing people, reading online, diving into data, and so forth. For others, you hold the content within your own head; the research involves getting those ideas out of the corners of your brain and into a project plan.

No matter what kind of research you need to do, don't put it off. Start digging into the topic as early as possible to get your background mental processes working.

Research Early

The Internet has created a growing industry of virtual assistants. You can hire people nearly anywhere in the world to undertake tasks for you while you do other things.

The catch with hiring any virtual assistant is that you have to organize the tasks for them to do. You must do some up-front work to save time in the end.

Your brain has its own network of virtual assistants ready to do your bidding, via the incubation effect described in chapter 12, When Will It Be Done. These mental processes work on your topic while you're doing other things. When you're ready to draft, they provide ideas. But they cannot get started until you give them something to work on. You do this by immersing yourself in thinking about the project. In other words, feed them with research.

If you have seven days scheduled for a project, research on day one, even if you don't plan to start writing until day five. Your mind can work on the subject while you're doing other things.

- Drifting off during a meeting? Ponder the subject of your writing project.
- Sitting on the train during the commute home? Let your mind wander back to your project.
- Walking the dog? Think about your audience avatar and their problems for a moment.

These small reminders bring up the project and refresh your neural networks.

Perhaps you'll get a flash of insight or think of an intriguing connection or angle. When you're ready to create the outline or start drafting, you'll have rich mental fodder ready to use. The words or ideas should come easily.

When *You* Are the Research Source

For some projects, you are the primary source of content. Even then, schedule time to research. In this situation, the inner research involves thinking deeply, taking notes, and gathering your thoughts.

Because finding the space to think about a topic can be a challenge, consider linking inner research with other activities.

For example, use a freewriting exercise to trigger inner research. Open a file, give it a temporary name, and start writing everything you can think of about the topic. When you run out of thoughts, keep going. Picture the audience avatar and come up with their questions.

At the end, highlight the key points that you want to cover in the finished result. Now, even if you put the project away for a while, you've encouraged your brain to ruminate on it. You might come up with questions that require external research.

If you're more comfortable speaking than writing, record your thoughts on the topic. The act of speaking about it will also get the virtual assistants in your brain working on the subject.

How Much Research Should You Do?

An experienced professional writer posed this question about research: "How do you gauge when enough research is enough? How do you know when you're researching as a method of procrastination, versus adding value to the finished product?"

Research can be enticing.

Excessive research is a dangerous form of procrastination. To anyone looking at you, you're working on the project, making progress. You might enjoy digging in and learning more.

How much is enough? When it comes to research, find the balance.

Here's my mantra: Seek to understand the subject one layer deeper than you need to. If you do this:

- You'll have a better idea of the questions to ask of experts or others.
- You'll learn where the pitfalls lie so you can avoid them. For example, you won't innocently choose an example that leads the reader to an unexpected complication.

"One layer deeper" is a subjective measure. Plan to gather more than you'll use, but within the scope needed for the project. Don't get stuck in perpetual research.

For lengthy works like books or reports, research may continue while you are drafting. The acts of outlining and writing often suggest avenues of questioning and additional investigation.

To fully understand a topic, write about it.

Once you have enough to sketch an outline, move on.

Chapter 14

The Writing Blueprint

Lay out your plans for the overall structure or outline before you start to draft.

If the word *outline* summons images of roman numerals and the essay form from school, let it go. For our purposes, the outline could be anything, including:

- A mind map created in software, on paper, or drawn on a whiteboard
- A series of notes or cards arranged in a particular order
- A bulleted list of points to cover
- Scribbled notes that only you can decipher. (That's my personal favorite for short pieces, but I have to move quickly before I forget what my notes mean.)

For a short blog post, start with an idea of how everything will fit together: the key points to make, in what order, and how you might hook the reader at the start.

My friend Karen Catlin, an author and coach for women in technology, suggests writing blog posts "tweet-first." She drafts three tweets summing up the key points she plans to make in the post, before she begins writing. By composing those tweets first, she narrows in on the points of the post and why she thinks someone would want to read it. Plus, there's an added benefit: once she publishes her blog post, she's prepared to start tweeting immediately.

The process of outlining makes you think through the topic, considering the ideal reader and the objective. You may discover areas of additional research or potential problems now. This will save you endless time when writing.

Outlines provide a necessary starting point, even if you abandon them partway through the first draft.

For longer content, the outline is a map that lets you write sections without regard to their linear order. You don't have to start at the beginning and work through to the end if that's not the way you're primed to write. You can skip around, as long as you fill in all of the structure by the time you're done.

Be aware that the process of composition often derails outlines. Writing is a golden opportunity to think intently about a topic, shutting out distractions. That deep thought may lead to ideas that change the course of the final product, in a positive way.

You may discover partway through that your outline doesn't work well.

> Don't be afraid to abandon or rework the outline as you draft.

Chapter 15

Find Your Writing Zone

Programmers and coders speak of working "in the zone," when the sense of time recedes and they become absorbed in the task at hand.

Psychologists refer to this as *flow*. It is the ideal state for *any* type of creative work, including writing, coding, painting, playing an instrument, or designing complex system architectures. We may do our best work when we're in the zone.

> Flow is the ultimate employee benefit.

You cannot force a state of flow, but you can set up the ideal conditions for it. If you find flow in other areas of your life, consider how you might create a similar environment for your writing.

According to Mihaly Csikszentmihalyi, the psychologist who literally wrote the book on the topic, nine elements must be present to realize a state of flow:

1. Work that is challenging but within your abilities
2. Clear goals

3. Immediate feedback through the activity itself

4. *Complete focus on the action*

5. *Functioning without distractions or mind wandering*

6. *Absence of fear of failure*

7. *Lack of self-consciousness*

8. Losing track of time passing

9. Fulfillment or enjoyment

Take a look at items four through seven on that list: focus on the action, lack of distraction, absence of fear, and lack of self-consciousness. We *can* control these variables during the drafting phase by inhabiting the right external environment and internal mindset.

Unfortunately, the modern work environment throws barriers in our way.

Maintaining a complete focus on the task at hand is difficult in an open-floor-plan office, for example. People and conversations may interrupt or distract you. Technology imposes its own, addictive demands for attention, enticing you to check every incoming email or ping. Workplace culture may instill fear of failure and self-consciousness about writing performance.

Pay attention to these factors when preparing to draft. Two of the core components of flow are "complete focus" and "lack of distractions." To be in the zone, you need to be able to focus on the work, without distractions. Find a way to make that happen.

Find the Environment That Works for You

You probably already know the conditions that set you up for optimal work.

Many writers who work in open offices use large, noise-cancelling headphones, not only to silence the sounds, but also as a visual signal that they are focusing, to prevent casual interruptions. Some people head home when they have to write, because the office has too many distractions.

Few of us can inhabit the perfect environment all the time.

When you're in the drafting phase, you may need to isolate yourself from your daily environment. Changing physical locations can be a useful mental trigger that you are doing a special kind of work. Consider finding an empty conference room or vacant office, a coworking space or the local library.

Once in your ideal spot, eliminate potential distractions from the outside world and from yourself.

The outside world may come into your writing space courtesy of your cellphone, smart watch, and browser tabs. Turn off all but the most critical applications.

The inner distractions are tougher to filter out. A stray thought sends you checking the calendar for a future appointment, or looking up a fact only to get lost in a swirl of emails or interesting blog posts.

Set a timer for the writing session, for anywhere from twenty-five to sixty minutes. Whenever you think of any small thing you need to do other than the writing, write it down and put it aside until after the timed session is done.

Revisit Your Objective, Audience Avatar, and Reader's Reason

Before starting the first draft, think once again about the purpose for the piece. Summon the audience avatar that you plan to use when drafting. See the person you plan to address in your mind's eye.

Having the audience in your mind will help you achieve a conversational tone and remind you to keep their needs in mind as you write.

Ready? It's time to start drafting.

Chapter 16

The First Pass

Keep two goals in mind during the drafting phase:

1. Creating a first, workable draft of a piece that will meet the audience needs (after revision)
2. Getting through the drafting phase as quickly and easily as possible

Don't aim for final or near-final copy at this point. Give yourself permission to finish this phase with a clumsy, awkward document you wouldn't show to anyone. You'll fix the problems during the revision stage.

Productive writers resist the urge to polish while writing the rough draft.

Drafting and revision use different mental processes. When drafting, your associative, nonlinear thought processes contribute words and examples. When revising, you judge and filter those contributions.

Faced with a critical inner editor, the associative, creative parts of your brain may stop contributing. When this happens, the work becomes slower and less pleasant. Every word is a struggle.

Worse, you may end up agonizing over word choice and sentence structure for text that you later cut. You waste precious mental cycles on words that disappear.

To write the first draft as quickly as possible, divide this phase into two passes:

1. In the first pass, build out the overall flow and structure, working rapidly and skipping over parts that give you trouble.
2. Use the second pass to fill in gaps, create transitions, and add detail or nuance.

For most people, the first pass is the hardest part.

Getting the Words to Flow

Once you've set yourself up to get in the writing zone, start writing. Begin whether or not you feel inspired or in the mood. Inspiration tends to follow action, not precede it.

Write through your outline in any order, starting with the sections that you feel ready to compose or that seem easiest.

If you're a particularly conscientious person, you may have a habit of doing the hard, unpleasant tasks first and saving the fun stuff for later. In many areas of your life, that habit serves you well. You're probably saving for retirement, too.

In this situation, however, don't put aside the best for last. Draft the parts that you're excited to work on right away. The act of writing may generate fresh perspectives on the parts that you are less certain about.

Write in any order, and don't polish or perfect yet.

If you're having trouble getting started, try these techniques to get the words flowing:

1. Conduct an inner conversation
2. Speak the draft to yourself
3. Enlist a listener

Conduct an inner conversation: The inner conversation method works best if you type or write quickly enough to keep pace with your thoughts. Here's how it works when typing:

1. Open a file and call it "zero draft" or "rough notes." The name signals that the contents of this file are not ready for external publication.
2. Think of a person from the target audience. Envision the audience avatar if you have one.
3. Look at your objective and outline, and start writing as if you were speaking directly to that person.

Write without worrying about word choices, editing, or revising. If you get stuck, leave a comment in the text and skip ahead. You can fix it later. When you're done, you'll have the first pass of the rough draft.

Speak the draft: Perhaps you would rather *talk* about your topic than write about it.

Find a place where you can speak without feeling self-conscious or bothering those around you. Record yourself speaking, then listen to it and type up the parts that work. Or use real-time voice-recognition software to capture and translate your spoken thoughts into written words.

Hint: If dictating with voice-recognition software, consider standing across the room, using a headset with your phone or a portable microphone. Otherwise, you could get distracted watching the words appear.

For many people, speaking gets the words flowing and activates a conversational tone. Use this strategy to talk through all the parts of the outline, in any order, and create the rough first pass.

You'll have to correct any oddities of the transcription technology and clean up the imperfections in your words. (We don't generally speak in grammatically correct sentences. Listeners fill in many gaps.) Read through and revise the text, fixing the flow of sentences, until the draft works as a written piece.

Enlist a listener: Genuine conversation involves more than one person. If the words don't come freely when you are alone, bring in another person to take the place of the reader.

When the audience is physically present, you benefit from nonverbal feedback. You can sense when the listener is bored, confused, or has questions.

To use this method:

1. Ask a colleague or friend to sit in for your target audience. Make sure they understand their role. (Bonus points if you can get someone from the actual target audience.)
2. Record the conversation to refer to later.
3. Talk through the outline that you plan to cover. If it's appropriate, draw pictures or use screen shots to illustrate points. Take notes of where you go astray, what questions came up, or where the outline doesn't work.

4. When you're finished, review what you have done. While it's fresh in your head, write up the first pass based on the conversation.

Bonus: Ask a new hire to take the role of the target audience. Tell them that they can impress you by providing a fresh perspective and asking questions, not by demonstrating what they know.

What to Do If You're Stuck

During the first, quick pass, you may gloss over parts that you're not sure how to handle. If you hit a roadblock or cannot continue, set your mental virtual assistants to the task.

To activate the incubating powers of your brain, wrestle with the problem for a while, then go do something else.

Your brain automatically reserves background cycles for unfinished work, like an unsolved problem. This is a variation on the incubation effect, and you can use it to your advantage.

For this strategy to work, you must consider the task *unfinished*. Remind yourself of the unsolved problem. Make a note of unresolved issues and scan them when you leave the desk or stop working.

Go do something entirely different. Ideally, find an activity that doesn't require deep focus and therefore allows your mind to wander. These might include:

- Sitting on a train
- Playing fetch with the dog
- Sitting in a particularly boring meeting (although this is not recommended if the meeting is important)

• Washing the dishes

When you are in this state, gently remind yourself of the problem. Don't try to solve it—just bring it back into your thoughts. You may come up with a metaphor that would explain a complicated concept, or a novel way to approach a topic.

Maybe no grand idea arrives. That's OK, you've still been setting the associative parts of your brain to work on the task. By doing so, you've increased the chances that they'll contribute words or ideas the next time you work.

This strategy works well for *any* creative endeavor, including solving scientific, mathematical, or coding problems. Give it a try.

Chapter 17

The Layering Pass

Claude Monet, a founder of French Impressionism, painted landscapes representing specific slants of light on scenes in nature. He would set up multiple easels next to each other, moving between them quickly to capture the changing effects of light on his subjects.

By all appearances, he worked quickly to capture a moment in time—the *impression* of the scene at that time. Some contemporary critics complained that the Impressionists did unfinished, shoddy work, without care or detail.

Monet's biographers reveal that after working outdoors, he took those canvases into his studio and continued adding layers and texture. His luminous compositions were built from thick layers of paint. Sections of his giant water lily canvases, painted in the last years of his life, include up to *fifteen* layers.

It's hard to create art that appears effortless.

As writers, we can do something similar. The Pulitzer Prize-winning journalist and writing teacher Donald Murray described *layering* his drafts, adding detail and texture to the text in the same way that Monet added layers of paint to his canvases. As Murray writes in *Writing to Deadline*, "Layering is especially helpful for journalists who have the time to work on the long piece in which tone and texture are important."

If you have followed the advice of getting the words down quickly, the first draft you've created may be rough, filled with notes to yourself (*fix this*) and missing sections.

You're not done yet. Take a second pass to do your own layering.

Add Layers

Layering isn't revision. You're still writing the first draft, creating original content and ideas, working on the scaffold of words you've already constructed.

If possible, leave a slice of time before this second pass to take advantage of the incubation effect. At least, let it rest overnight. If there's no time for that, take a short break.

During the layering pass, work from start to finish so you can experience the reader's linear flow. As you read, see where you might add research, explanation, stories, metaphors, or details.

If you were truly "in the zone" while drafting, you may have glossed over important sections or used terminology unknown to your reader. Thinking again about your ideal reader, consider whether you want to rearrange, add a story, or otherwise make the piece more compelling.

Although it would seem to prolong the drafting phase, adding a layering pass may help you be more productive because it frees you to work fluidly while drafting.

When you plan to take a second pass through the draft, you give yourself permission to write quickly during the first pass, while your brain is firing, just as Monet painted before the light faded. You ignore imperfections, because you know you will add layers and depth before revising and polishing. It's freeing.

Eventually, you've added enough layers to create a complete draft. Leave a slice of time so that you can rest, and then start revising.

Part Four:
The Revision
Process

Professional writers understand the importance of revision. If you care about the quality of your work, leave adequate time for revision in your project plans.

The length of the revision phase depends on many factors, including:

- Time available
- The state of the first draft
- Your standards (and latent perfectionism)
- The importance or permanence of the piece

Writers often underestimate the amount of time it takes to bring a rough draft up to their standards. Or, they draft until the last minute, stealing time from thoughtful revision. The work becomes frustrating.

Others can get stuck in perpetual revision. The inner perfectionist is afraid to let the work out into the world, and productivity suffers.

Neither path leads to success in the workplace.

To find the right balance, start with a clear objective. Approach the revision task with a well-defined plan, as described in the following chapters.

This section also discusses important issues to address in revision: terminology, grammar, and style.

Chapter 18

Why We Revise

Every writer in the workplace faces similar questions when revising their words:

- How much revision does this need?
- How much time am I willing to put into it?
- When is the piece "good enough"?
- Can I hand it off to someone else to edit, clean up, and take care of?

The only way to know when you've done enough is have a clear objective for the revision pass. Focus on what you're trying to achieve in the revision: the reader's fluency and comprehension.

> A piece is good enough when it works for the reader.

Revise for Cognitive Ease

According to the College Board, makers of Advanced Placement (AP) tests, the English Language and Composition test measures "reading comprehension of rhetorically and topically diverse texts." Put simply, stressed-out high school students are asked to read long, complicated passages and then answer questions about them.

The tests include excerpts from famous historians, scientists, politicians, and others, all respected as writers. The passages are chosen to induce *cognitive strain*. They are not inherently easy to understand.

Don't put your readers through a similar grind. In the business context, induce a sense of *cognitive ease*, making it as effortless as possible for readers to understand the text. The revision process is your best chance to eliminate cognitive strain.

Revision isn't about making yourself look good, or landing a spot as a featured author on an AP test.

Revise for the reader's sake.

If the topic you're writing about is complicated and dense, make sure that your words don't make understanding more difficult. Don't put cognitive hurdles in the reader's path. Word choices and sentence construction can either help or hinder comprehension.

The Reader's Brain

Combining written words into coherent sentences is a difficult task for computers, in part because many words have multiple meanings.

For example, the word *part* in the previous sentence could be a noun (be a *part* of something) or a verb (as in, *part* the Red Sea). In this case, it functioned as a component of the expression *in part.* Your brain probably figured that out quickly. Usually, the correct meaning is so obvious that we do not notice possible alternatives. This processing happens in the background.

A computer may iterate through a sentence several times to derive the right meaning. In developing programs that recognize spoken language, computer scientists and linguists have been learning from each other how we, as readers, decode the text that we read. Writers can benefit from these findings.

As we read, we navigate the different ways that a sentence could be assembled, and then put it all together to determine if it makes sense. We choose the most likely alternative for the sentence meaning and keep reading (or *parsing,* in computer terms).

If we reach a point at which the meaning isn't working, we stop, backtrack, and try an alternative meaning for what we've read.

Search out those places where someone might backtrack, so your readers don't encounter them.

Sentences that force readers to turn back are called *garden path* sentences. The name refers to the saying that to mislead someone is to "take them down the garden path." A classic example is:

The old man the boats.

When you reach *the boats,* you double back and realize that the subject is *the old* (as in old people) instead of *the old man.*

It only takes a moment. In that moment, you face unnecessary cognitive strain.

Every time we have to stop and reread, no matter how briefly, we disrupt the reading and comprehension process. We become less engaged with the *meaning* of the text, distracted by the effort to reassemble the sentences to make sense.

The curse of knowledge dictates that these garden path sentences will slip right past you as the writer, because you *know* what you were trying to say. You set out reading with the correct interpretation already in your mind.

External editors or third parties can find them more easily, but you should still search them out. By looking for problematic sentences during the revision phase, you practice getting outside your own head and into those of others.

What follows is advice for structuring your revision process to make the work fit your readers' brains.

Chapter 19

Top-Down Revision

Whether or not you enjoy revision, you don't want to spend more time than necessary in this phase of the work. Here's the secret to optimizing your revision process: start at the highest level and work your way in to finer detail.

By working from the top down, you prevent unnecessary detail work. For example, you could spend hours agonizing over word choices or rephrasing to avoid the passive voice in a section that you later decide is unnecessary. You cannot get that time back.

To protect your time, take a top-down approach to your revisions:

1. **First pass: objectives**. Evaluate the overall form, structure, and objective: Start at the beginning and read through to the end. Does the piece fulfill its objective? Do the headings and subheads guide the reader, and does the introduction pull the reader in?

2. **Second pass: flow**. Revise for the overall flow of the text. Are the sentences clear? Do people get stuck? Are there unnecessary abstractions?

3. **Third pass: details**. Now check the details. Look for punctuation, grammar, spelling, and word choice. Make adjustments for tone and style, and hunt out your specific writing mannerisms. Try reading aloud.

4. **Fourth pass: proofreading**. When the piece is in its final layout, get another person to proofread it.

Using this approach, you don't waste time with grammatical corrections in sections that you later cut or rewrite.

Four revision passes might sound like a lot of work to some writers, and not enough to others. Use your own judgment.

For a short piece, you might condense the second and third pass, cleaning up as you go. If you spot a typo while doing the first pass, make a note or fix it.

When the deadline is imminent, you may have to try to do them all at once.

If possible, leave time between the phases. Always leave time (or get a fresh set of eyes) before proofreading.

Revising with Editors

When working with editors, make sure they understand where you are in the revision process and what kind of edit you need.

For example, handle the first editing pass yourself if you feel that you are the best judge of the content and objectives. You might invite others to edit for flow, grammar, and style.

Conversely, you may ask for a third-party opinion on whether the argument makes sense, but retain control over the words themselves.

Proofreading can almost always be outsourced. A third-party proofreader usually does a better job than you can, because they do not "know" what the piece says. They see only what is actually on the page. The best ones train themselves to read this way, without getting caught up in the content or text.

Revising Writing Mannerisms

Your writing reflects your thought processes, which may be messier or more ambiguous than you would like the world to know.

You don't have to change the way you think, but you can easily control how your written words go out into the world, through a quick revision.

Learn to spot your particular thinking and speaking mannerisms. For example,

- Do you use "waffling" words like should, could, maybe, perhaps, some, just, simply?
- Do you default to boring adjectives like big, nice, or industry-leading?
- Do you emphasize points by adding really, very, actually, or other intensifiers? Removing these words makes the meaning stronger.

Likewise, if you write in a conversational style, speech mannerisms appear in the first draft. Phrases that sound casual in conversation appear timid in writing:

I thought that perhaps ...

I just wanted to ...

Do you mind ...

Take a clear-eyed look at your own work, or ask a friendly editor to identify unnecessary or weakening words in your writing. Make a list of the ones that appear frequently. This will be your personal "seek and destroy" list during revision.

In the third revision pass (details), search for those words and explore better ways to frame the sentence.

Chapter 20

Terminology, Abstractions, and Details

The Salesforce home page declares that the company is "the #1 CRM solution for small businesses." That's three abstract concepts (CRM, solution, and small business) and one detail: the ranking.

In business, technical, and scientific writing, the vocabulary that defines an industry can be a barrier to readers. Those of us doing the writing are too close to the words to see the problems.

Yet again, the curse of knowledge gets in the way. Once we've learned how people speak in our world, it's difficult to remember a time when we did *not* know the language.

As Steven Pinker writes in *The Sense of Style*: "The curse of knowledge means that we're more likely to overestimate the average reader's familiarity with our little world than to underestimate it."

If you think and write in the jargon of your field, revision is your chance to get outside your own head and take the reader's perspective.

Abstract Concepts

Abstract concepts are like parents—you love them and need them, but they can drive you nuts. (Not you, of course, Mom.)

Our brains use abstract concepts to make sense of our world. We encapsulate disparate ideas into larger containers: laptops and desktops roll up into the abstraction of *computer*; Microsoft and Salesforce are *software companies*, local mayors and heads of state belong to the broader category of *politicians*.

As we become adept at our jobs or expert in a field, we start *thinking* in abstract concepts and categories. Industry-specific terms become old friends that help us work through problems and communicate with each other quickly. Abstract thinking is the reason for the proliferation of industry jargon in the business world and in technical or scientific fields.

Because our written words reflect our thoughts, those same patterns turn up in our emails, web pages, investor reports, and marketing collateral—content that may reach people who *don't* know those terms. Even people within the industry may not know all of its jargon. If you're using the terminology as a way of assuming "insider" status, you might leave some readers feeling like unwelcome outsiders.

That's when abstraction becomes a problem. Revision is the cure.

The Three U's of Abstraction

Remember that the primary objective of revision is serving the reader. When communicating with people who don't share the same working vocabulary as you, take the extra effort to search out abstract concepts that are *unknown*, *unfamiliar*, or *unnecessary*.

Unknown: Has your target audience seen the term? Are you sure? Did you know this term when you started at your job? Would an intern starting in the role you are writing for know the term?

If the answer to any of these questions is *no*, either eliminate the term or define it.

Unfamiliar: Although you may be confident that a reader has been exposed to an abstract concept, take care. Readers who do not encounter and read the word regularly have to do the mental work of retrieving the meaning from memory. You are inducing a sense of cognitive strain. Readers might get bored and tune you out.

Unnecessary: Familiar, well-known abstract concepts tend to be less interesting than details. To make the content more interesting, search for unnecessary abstractions and consider replacing them with representative details.

If you're not sure which category an abstract concept falls into, find a reasonable stand-in for your target audience and ask them: how would you define this term? If they cannot answer, then it's an unknown. If they struggle, then it's unfamiliar.

To protect readers, spell out acronyms the first time you use them. Offer a parenthetical definition of an industry term when it first appears. Even if readers already know the term, many will appreciate the reminder.

Pay particular attention to abstractions involving people. They make the tone and style impersonal. Although they serve an important purpose, terms like *user*, *employee*, and *management* can seem dehumanizing.

In your second or third revision pass, look for cases of the unknown, unfamiliar, or unnecessary abstraction.

Replacing Abstractions with Stories and Details

When we get comfortable wielding the terminology of our jobs, we forget that abstract concepts are *containers for details*. Without details, readers get bored. Make the concepts come to life with stories and details.

In many cases, you can replace an abstract concept with a specific case without losing any meaning.

- If you're writing content for employees, consider replacing "the employee" with "you" (referring to the reader).
- If you're using the phrase "social media channels" but really mean Facebook and Twitter, write Facebook and Twitter.

Adept fiction writers understand the importance of the telling detail. Specific examples or images allow readers to construct the scene or setting in their own minds.

You can do the same with nonfiction business writing.

For example, an EPA document about Community Culture and the Environment offers stories about volunteers who monitor leaks of raw sewage into local streams. Raw sewage is a specific and memorable detail.

We don't remember data, but we do remember stories. When talking about the economy on the campaign trail, politicians tell stories about specific people they've met to illustrate data.

In his books *Liar's Poker*, *The Big Short*, and *Flash Boys*, author Michael Lewis explains the worlds of bond trading, real estate derivatives, and high-speed trading. These are complicated subjects filled with specialized terminology. Yet he brings the topics to life by telling the stories of the people involved, which compel us to understand the more complex topics. Stories work.

Chapter 21

Grammar Matters

Whether you're writing an email to a colleague or a report going out into the world on behalf of your business, take a moment to check and fix the grammar. (If you're already a grammar maven, reading this chapter may make you feel better about yourself. But I invite you to skip ahead if you'd prefer.)

Grammar matters for two reasons.

First, standard grammar is a courtesy to the reader. In most cases (and there are exceptions), sentences that obey common-usage grammar rules are easier for readers to understand.

Writing is all about communicating. A grammar check uncovers places where your words may lead the reader astray. If the subject and verb don't line up, or if you have a dangling modifier, the reader has to stop and decode what the sentence really means. Unnecessary cognitive strain may get in the way of communication.

Most grammar rules exist for reasons of clarity. Grammar represents the rules that our brains use for decoding language.

Second, in the business environment, grammar is part of the overall brand. Your brand isn't only the colors and fonts, or a clever tagline. It's the mental impression that others form when they encounter you or your business. The way you use language affects your perceived brand.

Most of us have a sliding scale of tolerance for grammar mistakes. We expect sentence fragments in tweets or short social media posts. We understand and read past errors in real-time messaging applications like Slack or text messages. And we'll give a writer leeway on quick email messages. (The "sent from my phone" disclaimer at the bottom of these messages is a plea for understanding and forgiveness.)

In other situations, readers are less forgiving.

What should I think if I find an obvious mistake in a business communication that you wrote? Consciously or not, I jump to one of the following conclusions:

- You don't know grammar; you lack sufficient education. (If, however, I know that you're not writing in your native language, I might not be as negative.)
- You're in a hurry and don't have the time to fix the grammar. This implies either overwork or poor planning.
- You don't care enough to check for obvious mistakes. (People who use spelling checkers regularly are less tolerant of mistakes that a spell check would find.)

Let's look at how these assumptions reflect on your personal or business brand.

- Insufficient education? You wouldn't put that on your LinkedIn profile.

- Overworked and in a hurry? Customers, investors, partners, and others beyond the business want to think you've got things under control.

- Not caring about details? Even a self-described "big picture" thinker should care enough to double-check the details.

Your default writing grammar isn't destiny. You can retrofit correct grammar in the revision phase, often by rephrasing sentences. If it doesn't come easily to you, use software tools or enlist outside resources.

Here's my quick guide to dealing with grammar in the revision.

Fit the Rule to the Usage

When I speak about grammar, I'm not referring to the rules you were taught in high school, like "Never end a sentence with a preposition." Fit the functional grammar of the writing to the style and audience. Write in a way that people can easily understand.

In most business situations, a conversational style of writing is appropriate. To test if the piece is working, read it aloud. Does it make sense? Ask someone else to read it aloud and check whether they deliver the intended meaning.

A sentence can follow all the rules of proper grammar and still sound awkward or be difficult to decode.

Language evolves with usage. Here are a few of the things that you were taught in school that may not make as much sense today.

Prepositions. It's OK to end sentences with prepositions. Example: "Where are you from?"

Conjunctions at the start of a sentence. Beginning sentences with words like *And* or *But* works in a conversational tone. But don't overdo it.

Insisting on "whom" for the object of a verb. Writing "whom" may sound pretentious in some situations. Consider rephrasing.

If you cannot break these rules, take the wise writer's way out: rephrase.

When in Doubt, Rephrase

When I'm writing fluidly, the words come out exactly as I think them. As it turns out, my thought processes are convoluted and indirect. My first-pass documents are often filled with stuffy, obtuse text that sounded brilliant in my mind but terrible when read aloud.

I can almost always find a simpler way to say something.

Avoid wading into a grammar controversy by writing clear, concise sentences. Rephrase, then rephrase again. Picture the target reader and write as you would speak to them.

Try reading your piece out loud, quickly and fluently, as if reading a teleprompter without knowing the text ahead of time. Where do you trip up? Did you get bogged down, or have to stop and take another run at a sentence? Consider revising, clarifying, or shortening that part.

Abide by the Unbreakable Rules

Many grammar rules protect the reader's understanding and should not be broken lightly.

For example, using *its* instead of *it's* can cause a moment of confusion on the part of the reader. This common mistake still makes me stop in my tracks while reading. (Helpful hint: Use the apostrophe when the word is a contraction of "it is." The possessive has no apostrophe: *his, hers, its.*)

Despite the fact that it drives me nuts, I often make this same mistake when drafting. My brain and fingers operate faster than my inner grammar maven. Everyone makes errors. I try to be forgiving of others and myself.

The longer the work, the tougher it is to eliminate all the problems. I find typos, spelling errors, and other issues in books by well-known authors, produced by major publishing houses. Despite going past two excellent professional editors, *this* book will undoubtedly have a glitch or two. (They're my fault, since I keep fiddling with the words.)

Grammar isn't about being smarter or better than anyone else. It's about communicating with the fewest possible problems.

Automated Tools and Human Editors

Software is an excellent first line of defense in the search for grammar problems.

Most writing software includes a spell checker. Use it. The spell checker cannot detect when you use the wrong word, correctly spelled, but it can save you the embarrassment of many misspellings.

Microsoft Word also includes a grammar checker. Although easily foiled by product names or industry-specific usage, it still catches a great deal. If the grammar checker burps on a sentence, pay attention. Even if you are certain that the sentence is correct, your readers may trip up in the same place.

You can find numerous free and paid grammar checkers online. Many writers rely on Grammarly, which claims to catch hundreds of problems that Microsoft Word cannot. You can upload documents to the application or use the browser extension to check your writing in LinkedIn, emails, blog posts, and other online locations. Grammarly offers both free and paid versions.

After you've done automated checks, reread and check the piece yourself. Get someone to edit the work if it's important. You're writing for a human reader, so use a human editor when it counts.

Chapter 22

Style: Yours, Ours, Theirs

Your words reflect your thoughts to the world. Just as you pay attention to the clothes in which you dress yourself, take care with your writing style. It's how you present the inner workings of your mind.

Your writing style is a combination of two factors:

1. The way you think
2. Revision

Those authors who spin out beautiful prose are human beings, too. Do you imagine that their thought processes are less jumbled than your own? Perhaps. More likely, they have developed an effective writing style through ongoing work and careful revision. They weren't born writing that way.

When creating content at work, you might switch between three distinct writing styles:

1. *Your personal style*: Your own voice, used when writing for people who know you.

2. *Industry style*: The voice of your role in the company or industry. Your personal voice is subdued when writing in the industry style.

3. *Brand style*: The voice of the business or company. Your personal style generally disappears entirely.

All three variations of style deserve attention.

Your Personal (Work) Style

Your written words take your place when you're not present.

Wear hoodies and T-shirts in the office if that's your style. Be informal with your teammates if that's the workplace culture. But when you write a product brief or strategy document, tidy up your style. The phrases that sound casual, ironic, or witty when spoken one-on-one may undermine your credibility when written and distributed.

Psychologists have proved that in personal conversations, we derive a great deal of meaning through tone of voice and body language. Written words lack your physical presence. In the absence of body language and auditory clues, readers interpret meaning and intention from the words alone.

In that context, your words may broadcast signals you don't want to send. For example, the presence of extraneous words can come across as uncertainty, lack of confidence, or unclear thinking.

If you care about how you are perceived at work, on your next writing project remember to do a quick revision to check the tone and style. Present a slightly better version of yourself.

Beware of weasel words. The term *weasel word* refers to words or phrases used to intentionally add ambiguity to a statement, disguising its true meaning.

For example, the employee being laid off is *downsized*, while the passenger violently ejected from a plane is *re-accommodated*. When using those words, you are making an intentional decision to gloss over reality.

However, you may sprinkle your writing with small, unintentional weasel words that erode meaning or diminish the strength of your statements. They include *kind of, sort of, somewhat, perhaps, some, just,* and *simply.*

Because we write as we think, our words reflect passing doubts, uncertainties, and distracting thoughts. We lace our writing with words and phrases that undermine our meaning.

Removing those words strengthens the prose.

Read through your writing, looking for these qualifiers. Chances are, you regularly rely on two or three words or phrases that dilute your style. Once you know your personal favorites, do a global search for them before sending your writing out to others.

Yes, it takes time to edit them out. Think of it as an investment in your career—particularly if you're a woman working in a male-dominated field. Little weasel words and phrases erode your credibility.

If you are genuinely uncertain about something, don't make the reader guess about it. Bring the unknowns to the forefront.

For example, in a project-planning document, collect the issues you're not sure about and put them under a heading that invites others to contribute, such as "Missing pieces" or

"As yet undetermined." Instead of apologizing for what you don't know, you're inviting collaboration. There's a world of difference.

Use fewer words for greater impact. For most of us, revision is a process of elimination. Get to the point, lead with what the reader needs to know, and cut extra words.

Your readers will thank you, and you will appear competent and confident.

The Industry Style

When writing in the voice of your role, you adopt the vocabulary, tone, and style of the industry. Don't get carried away with sounding like everyone else.

Style can be a way to broadcast an insider status. For example, some authors adopt a formal and complex style to signal education level, background, or intelligence. In disciplines such as academia and the law, the industry style is like a credential. But when lawyers write text for a general audience, they often sound like the disclaimers at the end of drug commercials: wordy and convoluted. The style should match audience expectations.

Research shows that readers aren't impressed by fancy vocabulary and verbal complexity.

In 2006, Daniel Oppenheimer, then a professor of psychology at Princeton University, tested the thesis that a more sophisticated vocabulary earns greater respect from readers.

Originally published in the journal *Applied Cognitive Psychology*, his paper illustrates its thesis in its own title: "Consequences of Erudite Vernacular Utilized Irrespective of Necessity: Problems with Using Long Words Needlessly." The paper went on to win the coveted Ig Nobel Prize (*not* to be confused with the Nobel Prize). The Ig Nobel Prize, bestowed by the website Improbable Research, honors "research that makes people laugh, and then think."

The researchers tried many tactics to test responses to writing complexity. In one experiment that hits home for English majors everywhere, they prepared personal statements for candidates for admissions to English Literature studies at Stanford University. They then created a more complex version of each statement by replacing nouns, verbs, and adjectives with longer synonyms.

The researchers asked readers to evaluate the statements and the authors, rating how likely they would be to recommend the authors for admission to graduate programs. As expected, the readers rated the more complicated statements as being more difficult to read.

Here's the key point: increasing written complexity *lowered* the evaluators' estimation of the applicant's intelligence. The "smarter" the vocabulary, the less intelligent the writer appeared.

In another test, the researchers found two different, published translations of the same passage written by René Descartes, a French philosopher and mathematician with enormous influence on Western thought.

One of the translations used longer, more complex words than the other. Again, evaluators were asked what they thought of the intelligence of the author (not the translator). Some evaluators were told that the original author was Descartes.

As you might now expect, those who read the simpler version rated the author as more intelligent compared with ratings of the more complex translation. This was true even when readers were told that the author was Descartes and the text a translation.

Think about that for a moment. A stuffy translation knocks a few points off Descartes's perceived IQ.

As readers, when we have to work hard to make sense of text, we don't feel less intelligent. No, we decide that *the author* is less intelligent. As Oppenheimer writes, "Simpler writing is easier to process, and studies have demonstrated that processing fluency is associated with a variety of positive dimensions."

> The harder readers have to work, the less they think of the author.

People will think you are smarter if you make them feel intelligent by clearly explaining complicated topics. That's the most compelling argument I can offer for writing simply and clearly.

The Brand Style

Your personal style disappears entirely as you write in the voice of the company, the brand, or another executive. In these cases, you'll need to understand the brand's tone and style.

Write the piece first, then go through the brand's style guide and see what you need to change.

You don't have a style guide? Say it's not so!

Remedy that situation by reading chapter 26, The Style Guide Is Your Friend. Until you can get one together:

- Look around for the most successful pieces—website copy, email promotions, presentations—and try to emulate the style. Consistency across communications is important for content that leaves the business.
- With no other direction, attempt a neutral but conversational style. You may end up creating the brand tone and style yourself.

The Conversational Style

Because we spend our lives conversing with others, a conversational writing style is easy for people to absorb.

Most business writing benefits from a conversational tone and style. This is particularly true of text that people read online, including:

- Blog posts
- Website copy
- Ebooks

However, creating conversational style when writing isn't as easy as talking.

> Spoken speech and written speech are not the same.

If you have ever read a verbatim transcript of an interview, or listened carefully to a recording of a real-world conversation, you already know that few of us speak in perfect prose. Our sentences ramble on, or we stop in the middle as another thought interrupts us. It doesn't work on paper.

Likewise, we may string together long, grammatically complex constructions with many clauses when speaking. We supplement the words with body language, vocal inflection, facial expressions, and the overall spark of communication between individuals. These clues help a listener understand our meaning.

A reader doesn't have the advantage of your inflection and gestures. You cannot see in their eyes when they are confused, and respond accordingly. The written word holds the entire burden of the communication.

When possible, use simple sentence constructions and shorter paragraphs, giving the reader a chance to pause and process concepts as they read.

Part Five:
The Review Process

Once you've revised the work, there's usually one more step before the final product is done: showing it to other people. If the work needs the approval of others in the business, pay attention to the chapters in this section. Many worthy projects have suffered a lonely death in a lingering, drawn-out review process.

Your productivity is measured by how many projects are completed and published. Without approvals, you will be an unproductive writer.

The approval process may be simple, with only one individual signing off, or the whole team might weigh in. Unless you're the only person who approves content, the chapters in this section can help you get through this phase quickly.

This step might feel like an awkward hurdle between you and the finish line. If not managed well, external reviews can be painful. You may feel like others are taking potshots at your hard work. You may be tempted to wash your hands of the piece once it enters review, leaving it to editors to take the work to publication.

The review phase is a valuable opportunity to observe how well the piece works outside your own head. Reviews are a chance to defeat the curse of knowledge and serve the reader with effective content. They are a critical part of the writing process.

The chapters that follow offer guidelines for making the most of the approval and review process through:

- Careful planning
- Explicit review requests
- A strategy for integrating feedback

Because tone and style are often sticky issues during reviews, this section also includes advice on creating a corporate style guide.

Chapter 23

Start with a Plan

You've almost made it to the finish line, but until the work is approved, you're not quite done.

The review process postpones getting the work into the world. Yet it often adds value to the finished work, and serves the reader well.

Make a plan and take charge. Start with clear objectives.

Review Objectives

Like the project itself, the review process may have several objectives, including:

- Ensuring that the finished product meets the needs of the target audience
- Confirming the accuracy of the subject matter
- Avoiding legal liability
- Getting the necessary approval and sign-offs to publish by a deadline or as quickly as possible

If you have multiple objectives, consider splitting the review process into phases: collecting feedback from target readers or subject matters experts first, then getting the sign-off from approvers.

Doing a phased review often simplifies the reviewer's work. However, it may lengthen the total elapsed time before publication. Manage the timeline carefully.

Use Reviews to Defeat the Curse of Knowledge

Business writers must align the content with the reader's cognitive background, defeating the curse of knowledge described in chapter 4. The easier it is for readers to understand the text, the better they will feel about you or your business.

Use the external review process to get a fresh perspective on the readability and effectiveness of the content. Look for people who can represent the target audience. Ask them to find the places in the piece where they want further clarification, or where they get bogged down.

Unless you explicitly ask people to report their moments of confusion, many will gloss over them. They may not want to offend you by pointing out awkward sentences. Perhaps they feel like they *should* know what you were trying to say. Many reviewers only check to see that the writing is grammatically correct, then keep going.

Text can be grammatically correct and yet be brutal to hack through. You need a higher standard than "correct."

Find one or two people you trust and ask them to mark any glitches they encounter while reading with a highlighter, comment, or question. Their targets include:

- Sentences that they had to read twice to understand
- Terminology or phrases that make them pause or look for context
- Anything that they did not understand or words they had to look up
- Metaphors or stories that didn't make sense

These are the places where the curse of knowledge is erecting barriers to comprehension. When you get the review copy back, consider rephrasing or reworking those parts. Provide clarification where possible.

Distinguish Between Review and Approval

You might ask different people to contribute in unique ways to the review process, including subject matter experts, legal teams, and editors. Their feedback may spur further changes to the piece.

Wait until you've integrated feedback related to content, tone, and style before you send out the copy for final approval. Then, ask the approvers to either sign off or make specific objections.

Your plan might look like this:

1. *Review phase one*: Ask for feedback, suggestions, areas that need clarification, and content checks
2. *Revision*: Incorporate any feedback from the first phase
3. *Review phase two*: Ask for approval
4. *Revision*: Incorporate final feedback if necessary

An approver who also offers feedback might look at the piece twice—during the first phase and for a final sign-off.

Schedule Sufficient Time

A schedule may be more important during review than at any other point in the process. As review cycles drag on, people have opportunities to change their minds about the objective or execution. In this situation, time is your enemy.

Create and enforce a schedule for the reviewers and approvers. Give them deadlines.

How much time you give reviewers depends on the length of the piece and how motivated people are to take action.

Deadlines add urgency, so use them.

While lengthy content should have longer review processes, don't give people too much time. Here are typical guidelines:

- A blog post: a day
- A five-page paper: two or three days
- A twenty-page paper: one week

Unless a reviewer is traveling or unavailable, don't allow more than a week. Most people will delay the work until the last day, no matter how much time they have.

Approvals should require less time than content reviews or edits. Ask for approvals within two days.

Leave time in the schedule for integrating the revisions, as well as any final copyediting and proofreading before publication.

Chapter 24

Know How to Ask

Do not send your blog post, article, position paper, script, proposal, or chapter draft out into the cold, cruel world of external reviews without a well-defined set of directions. Provide guidelines for each reviewer, including the following three pieces of information:

1. Objective of the piece (including target audience)
2. The reviewer's obligations for this cycle
3. A specific deadline

Start with the Project Objective

Along with the content, include a summary of the target audience and the purpose of the piece from the planning phase in Part Two. This information provides critical context for the reviewer.

If you took the extra step of getting sign-off on those objectives before starting, include that in the review guide. ("As you'll remember, the executive team agreed to this plan last week.") This discourages people from rethinking the whole project.

People who have agreed to the objective and audience in advance are less likely to derail a project during reviews.

Clarify the Reviewer's Tasks

Be explicit about what you are asking of the reviewer, even if it seems obvious to you.

You might be surprised how many people in your workplace channel an inner editor or English teacher when you give them something to read. Suddenly you find yourself having discussions about passive voice, semicolons vs. em dashes, or paragraph length with people you were turning to for legal advice.

Let people know exactly what kind of feedback you need from them.

Setting clear expectations may result in a faster turnaround. If you hand someone a ten-page position paper to review, she may put it off for later. If you tell her, "I need you to check the description of the API on page six," she might do it immediately. You get a quick response and she doesn't add the project to the to-do pile.

Send different instructions based on the reviewer's role, such as:

- Reviewers reading for flow and fluency
- Subject matter experts
- Approvers: people who own the strategy or technology and need to sign off

- Copyeditors or proofreaders responsible for fixing errors without changing content

Although adding instructions takes a few extra minutes while sending out material for review, it streamlines the overall process. It's time well spent.

Set Explicit Deadlines

Describe the deadline with a specific date and time. Many email programs and smartphones highlight dates for a quick addition to the calendar. Write the deadline clearly, so that it shows up as a potential one-click calendar entry.

To add urgency, let people know the importance of the deadline. For example:

- Describe what you will do if you don't get the review back by the deadline. If you can get away with it, consider turning a lack of response into tacit approval: "If I don't hear back from you, I'll assume that you're fine with the copy as it is."

- If you're in a rush but cannot proceed without a response, include a reason for the urgency: "If I get the comments back by Monday morning, we can meet our planned publication date of next Tuesday. Earlier is better, giving me more time to integrate the comments and proofread the final copy."

You can deliver this information verbally, then follow up with an email when you send the review. Here's an example.

"Hey, Max, here is the blog post we talked about, designed to encourage existing customers to try the new feature. Please confirm that the description of the technology is accurate. Let me know by tomorrow, Tuesday at 2pm, so this can go on the blog Wednesday. We won't publish it without your OK."

That email mentioned the objective, the audience, the reviewer's expectations, an explicit deadline, and a reason for urgency. Don't let it get lost in the inbox, either. Create an email subject line that communicates urgency. For example, the subject line of the email above might read, "Please confirm by 2pm Tuesday."

Send Reminders if the Schedule is Tight

Raise your hand if you've ever procrastinated on an important project. Yes, we all do. Other, urgent activities get in the way until the deadline is near.

Your reviewers may do the same thing.

Remind reviewers one day ahead of the deadline. Put an alert in your schedule to send a reminder or check in personally if you haven't received feedback or approval. Try it— you'll get more responses to review requests.

Chapter 25

Put It All Together

Here's how it's supposed to work: You ask for review comments. People send them in by your deadline. You integrate the comments and then finalize the piece.

That's the perfect world. In the real world, these things happen:

- You get no responses to the review request at all.
- You get conflicting review responses and have to decide which revisions to make.
- A reviewer threatens to derail the project with comments or input beyond what you were looking for.

Use the following advice for dealing with these common situations.

Nothing but Silence

Your request for reviews may meet with deafening silence.

You ping people the day before the deadline, and the response is the common refrain: "I don't have time to look at this now."

If you've framed the lack of response as implicit approval, you can proceed. Lack of feedback could be a positive sign that people trust you to do the right thing.

Perhaps you run out of time to wait for reviews; you can publish the work and fix it later if anyone finds a problem. This is the natural state of writing for the web, where updating content may take minutes.

If you need an approver's input to move forward, walk that fine line between stalking and bribing. Offer to bring them morning coffee if they'll take fifteen minutes to read the text. Leave notes on the windshield of their car. You're a writer—get creative.

If no one responds at all, you could take the path of least resistance and publish. But watch out: You haven't had the chance to defeat the curse of knowledge. You're missing the opportunity to improve the work, leaving it to readers to find the awkward parts. They may never let you know. They'll just stop reading.

A writing friend of mine puts it this way: "People are busy, and don't have time to review. That lets me be lazy."

If you work on a team, find a buddy and agree to review each other's pieces before they are published. Steal a practice from software engineering teams that require peer reviews before code can be pushed into production. Use the same practice for writing.

If you don't work on a team or cannot find anyone to fill this role, hire a freelance editor.

Bonus: Working with a good editor rubs off on you, gradually improving your writing as you internalize their input.

Conflicting Review Comments

If you planned in advance, you already know what to do when you get conflicting review comments. Otherwise, you'll have to use your judgment based on the situation.

If resolving the issue is outside your realm, ask for guidance: Who gets the upper hand in conflicts about partnerships? Legal terms? Technical content?

Instead of raising the specific issues under discussion, ask about the authority.

If you disagree with the comments, but the reviewer raises a legitimate issue or has authority over that area of the review, you may have to cede the point.

It's difficult to let go of attachment to your words, especially the parts you love. The sentences or metaphors that you feel the most strongly about may represent *your* worldview, not that of your audience.

Advocate for the reader, not your own words.

If reviewers suggest changes that serve readers in the target audience, respect the work enough to accept the changes. If you think the changes do not serve the reader well, then fight for their interests.

Rogue Reviewers

Reviewers may go beyond the scope of their responsibilities and, in doing so, threaten to derail the process.

The best way to prevent rogue reviewers is to clearly communicate your expectations when you ask for the review.

Now, I love it when *anyone* catches typos or grammatical mistakes, no matter what role they fill. But it's no fun getting into arguments about the serial comma with a software engineer, or discovering that a subject matter expert has a personal aversion to using the second person singular (you), despite the brand style.

Sometimes, people want to feel that they have left their mark on a project. They rewrite entire sections of a report or web page, often in a tone and style that does not match the rest of the document or website. What do you do?

If you have carefully communicated expectations for reviewers ahead of time, you have an out. "Thanks for the input. I'm incorporating your changes about the technical accuracy, and will take the rest into consideration."

If you can integrate some suggestions without affecting the quality of the final result, go ahead and do so. Heck, the person cares enough to do a review.

Remember, you're on a team. But always try to serve the reader first.

Beware of HiPPOs

If you do not have a plan in place ahead of time, then final authority on all conflicts defaults to the HiPPO: the Highest Paid Person in the Office.

Every designer has encountered the executive who exhibits newfound expertise in font choices and color theory during logo design. The same thing happens in writing. Founders or high-ranking executives may insist on personal preferences in outbound communications, sometimes against the advice of people they pay for advice or expertise.

It's not all bad. The high-ranking person generally cares about the work. Founders, for example, are personally and deeply invested in all aspects of the business. Their input is critical for strategic decisions.

For metaphors and word choice, however, their opinions may not align with the target reader. Unless you're writing for a target audience of CxOs, the highest-ranking person in the room frequently does not represent the ideal reader.

Creative work is subjective.

When in this situation, try to back up your position with external validation. Survey people in the target reader demographic. A customer advisory council can be invaluable. Run a test of the message with people outside your company. Sites like PickFu let you do A/B testing (comparing two variations) quickly and inexpensively.

Don't sabotage your career in the effort. If external confirmation doesn't sway the HiPPO, concede and move on knowing you have done your best.

The Unending Review

The worst possible fate for your written work is a review process that lingers, eventually stalling out after months or years.

If you have a review plan and communicate deadlines, you can usually get the job done. On occasion, however, events spin out of your control:

- A key participant or approver changes roles.
- Business priorities shift, reducing urgency for the project.
- People cannot resolve an essential conflict, and no one is backing down.

Know when it's time to move on.

Maybe you can salvage smaller projects from the work. Dig a blog post out of a failed report, or split the project into multiple smaller ones that can gain approval.

Some day you *will* work on a project that never reaches the finish line. It happens. Even the most successful and valued writers and team players strike out from time to time.

Chapter 26

The Style Guide
Is Your Friend

If you're writing content for external audiences, then you need a style guide.

The *AP Stylebook*, *Chicago Manual of Style*, and other standards are invaluable references, but they're not enough. They cannot answer the essential issues that people will argue about during revisions, such as:

This is too informal.

We shouldn't refer to our customers as users.

This sentence is too long.

To solve those thorny issues, you need a guide that's specific to your business.

> A style guide protects you from contentious revision cycles.

Why a Style Guide Saves You Time

I have worked with many start-ups over the years. Only a couple had corporate style guides. The rest worked so furiously churning out content in start-up mode that they couldn't take the time for the internal task of creating a style guide.

I'd often create one for them as a bonus, because I had to make judgments about style while writing anyway.

A style guide saves everyone time.

The process of creating a style guide can be fraught with tension or disagreement, particularly in large organizations. If people complain about how difficult it's going to be to create a guide, that's a sign that you need one.

The style guide consolidates all the disagreements and puts them to rest: *Argue once, write many times.*

If you work on your own within your team or organization, a style guide prevents you from becoming the repository of all things related to the corporate voice.

Don't be a human style guide.

Everyone wants to be needed. But if you're the only one who controls the corporate or brand style, you can quickly become overwhelmed. Every little thing needs your touch, distracting you from writing or other tasks. If you go on vacation, everyone panics.

A style guide externalizes insight and knowledge about the brand voice in a shareable document. You can give it to other writers or editors, freeing yourself to work on the fun projects.

Style guides enable a consistent tone and style across different authors and pieces. An effective style guide makes everyone productive.

The Minimum Style Guide

If your business does not yet have a style guide, you can assemble a basic version using the five components listed below.

1. Terminology, product names, and usages: Get everyone to agree on the key terms and usages in your business, as well as product names and categories. Can you make the product name plural, for example: Acme Gizmos? Is "backup" one word or two when it's a verb?

2. Voice: If you had to choose three adjectives to describe your business, what would they be? Given your three adjectives, determine how they affect the mechanics of the prose.

- Second person: Do you use "you" when referring to the reader, or do you prefer to write in third-party abstractions ("they")?

- First person plural: Do you refer to the business in the third person, or can you say "we" in writing? In which situations?

- Authoritative vs. collaborative: Do you want to be perceived as the font of authority, or do you want a conversational, we're-in-this-together style?

- Humor: Is humor appropriate, and if so, where and how much?

3. Punctuation: Decide whether you're adhering to the *AP Stylebook*, the *Chicago Manual of Style*, or another source as a final arbiter. Resolve the most common dilemmas so people don't have to hunt for them:

- Commas: Choose a side in the epic serial-comma debate. The serial comma is the last comma before the word *and* or *or* in a list of three or more items. I chose to use the serial comma in this book because it enhances clarity. It's a choice, not a lifestyle or religion.

- Dashes: If dashes are consistent with your corporate style, what size dash do you use? The em dash is longer than the en dash.

- Gender-neutral pronouns: Are you OK with using "they" to mean he or she? Do you try to alternate he and she in examples to imply neutrality? Or do you state up front that he can refer to either gender? The singular "they" is gaining ground in practice, particularly in informal writing. The editors of the AP Stylebook have recently ruled that the singular "they" is acceptable as a gender-neutral alternative "when alternative wording is overly awkward or clumsy." I've used it in this book because the style is conversational—have you noticed?

4. Capitalization: Which terms or common words should you capitalize? Legitimate candidates include:

- Product names
- Terms for which you have trademarks or registered trademarks
- Major words in headings (depending on your heading styles)

- Industry terms like "Internet" or "Wi-Fi"

Note that when it comes to capitalization, more is *not* better. When writing in English, don't capitalize words within sentences without good reason. All-capital text has almost no place outside headline copy. Everywhere else it looks like shouting.

5. Blacklisted words: Come up with a list of overused or stale words and ban them from your content. Anyone using a blacklisted word should present a convincing business case. My personal, marketing-related blacklist includes:

- Leading: This word is overused to the point of meaninglessness.
- Impactful: Its impact is to drive me crazy.
- Utilize: Most of the time, the word *utilize* serves as an ugly substitute for the simpler *use.*

Share your basic style guide with everyone who creates content on behalf the business, including bloggers, designers, and editors. Put a date on it. An effective style guide evolves over time.

You can include examples or detail, but avoid creating a long and complicated document. If you want people to use it, shorter is better.

The magazine *The Economist* publishes its style guide online. The introduction includes wonderful gems, like "Clarity of writing usually follows clarity of thought." Refer to it for inspiration.

Part Six: Troubleshooting Your Process

Having a solid process improves your chances of getting the job done quickly and with positive results. Unfortunately, process cannot guarantee success. The work environment throws unexpected and varied obstacles in our paths.

Preparing for this book, I spoke with many writers about the challenges they encounter. Although they worked in various jobs and diverse environments, the problems coalesce around certain themes. This section includes the most common issues:

- Finding the focus to work
- Pulling content from reluctant subject matter experts
- Dealing with a shrinking deadline
- Writing as a group or team
- Lack of recognition or attribution

There are no hard-and-fast rules for handling these hurdles, but the practices in the following chapters may help you make the best of whatever situation you encounter.

Chapter 27

Distractions and Focus

A writer in the workplace faces many competing demands.

If writing isn't the main part of your job but one of its many responsibilities, you have to carve out time and attention for the concentrated work of drafting while still managing the other work you are paid to do.

If your job title includes the word *writer*, the responsibilities typically extend far beyond the contemplative act of writing. This is how one of my friends describes her work as a writer at a major software company on her LinkedIn profile:

- Establish collaborative and effective relationships across creative, campaign, brand, and business unit teams
- Juggle highly visible initiatives, messaging, and writing for global product launches
- Craft and sell strategic messaging
- Deliver creative content that consistently drives qualified sales leads and builds engagement: campaign

themes, landing pages, microsites, banner ads, nurture emails, customer stories, video scripts, blogs, white papers, brochures, event support, press releases, social ads, auto-responders, sales materials, etc.

- Manage and mentor a junior writer

I'm exhausted just reading this. How does she find time to write?

Your success depends on how well you balance the competing demands of the external world (job responsibilities) and the inner one (the work of writing).

The answer lies in one word: *focus.*

Focus is how you direct your attention both beyond yourself and within, to the world and to the work. Mastery over focus plays a larger role in your career than mastery of grammar. Automated tools and third-party editors can fix your grammar. Only you can control your focus.

The physical work environment is the most obvious impediment to focus. With people popping by your desk or constant pings from online apps, it's impossible to find a state of flow when drafting, or to think deeply about the reader's perspective. Chapter 15, Find Your Writing Zone, discussed ways to get into the zone for writing. It's not always possible to escape the distractions.

Don't use the environment as an excuse for not writing. Our distractions often come from within.

> Focus is a battle fought on two fronts: external and internal.

We have to give up those apps that tempt us with immediate feedback or a sense of urgency, if only for a short time.

The fear of missing out on what's happening around us can prevent us from diving into the writing.

External Environment

Suppose that you do your best drafting in a quiet, uninterrupted spot, with soothing music in the background. At your desk in a humming office, you struggle to get into the zone. People stop by with questions. You hear conversations, or see a board member walking past and wonder if something is going on that you should know about.

This basically describes the plight of many writers on the job.

I asked a group of writers about how they find the focus to do their writing in the office. These are a few of their mechanisms for coping with the reality of the workplace:

- Block every Thursday morning from the schedule
- Work from a coffee shop
- Turn on music
- Write at home in the middle of the night
- Go hide in a conference room for an hour
- Come in to work early
- Come back to the office after the kids are in bed.

For many, the key to getting the job done is getting out of the office, or finding a way to work when no one is there.

If this sounds like your situation, consider the following advice.

Remember, the problem lies with the workplace, not you. One product manager at a high-tech company says she feels *less productive* than her colleagues because she cannot write in her open-floor-plan office. Instead, she spends Sunday evenings drafting blog posts and other content, feeling like it's her fault.

It's not her fault. It's the workplace.

Advocate for a better situation. As the list above indicates, the writers I queried came up with strategies for managing their environments: reserving conference rooms, blocking off parts of their calendar, or getting permission to work from home or a coffee shop regularly. They either sought permission or just made it happen. Your workplace should help you find a situation conducive to focus and writing.

The Inner Working Environment

The noisy demands of the workplace may push the quiet work of writing out of the way. Rather than resenting the interruptions, we may subconsciously welcome them. We may find it difficult to motivate ourselves to focus and start.

Cognitive scientists have identified several biases or mental habits that conspire against our writing plans:

- Because of the *present bias,* we tend to put off difficult projects for the future and pick easier, fun things to do immediately. (Procrastinators know what I'm talking about.)

- Because of the *planning fallacy,* we don't think anything will go wrong. We make overly optimistic plans, then put off the work in favor of other tasks that seem urgent.

- Technology exerts its addicting forces on us, calling us away from our thoughts. As Nir Eyal points out in

Hooked: How to Build Habit-Forming Products, the various apps and technologies in our lives are explicitly designed to be engaging and habit-forming.

We have to find creative ways to trick our unproductive selves into writing, working against these trends.

Here are a few strategies that might work for you.

Make plans and deadlines. We tend to work on the most urgent projects first. If we wait until the final deadline looms, we may short-change the drafting, incubation, and revision phases of the work. To realize the benefits of urgency without the downsides of stress and rushed writing, create individual deadlines for each phase of the work.

Categorize competing demands. If a writing project is one of twelve tasks on your to-do list for the day, there's a good chance you won't get to it. When it is one of three tasks, you have a harder time ignoring it.

Consider grouping the competing tasks into virtual buckets based on projects or your personal goals. If possible, stick to three main categories. Then tackle only *the most important* task from each bucket, rather than trying to check off as many items as possible.

Your top three categories may change from week to week, depending on what's going on at work and in your life. When a project is high priority, you might work only on that for a while.

As a valuable by-product of this exercise, you can identify neglected areas of your life. For example, if you have a category labeled *professional development* but spend all your time in the *administrative tasks* category, you may have a prioritization problem.

When you find yourself doing work that doesn't fit in *any* of your buckets, stop and ask yourself why you're doing it.

If the writing is important to you, personally or professionally, make sure you dip into the writing bucket on a regular basis.

Go on virtual lockdown. When you're sprinting to the finish on a project, try putting yourself in a virtual lockdown. This is one way to shift your mindset for a short period of time.

Some software companies use the lockdown model for engineering teams facing looming deadlines. When a team is in lockdown for a project, its members cannot be pulled into unrelated meetings, and don't have to do ordinary administrative tasks.

Lockdown mode shuts off competing distractions.

I use this strategy when working to meet a strict writing deadline. For me, lockdown means:

- Limiting extra activities, except those needed to maintain health and sanity
- Deferring or declining commitments to others
- Checking email less frequently
- Temporarily giving myself permission to ignore the many things I feel I should be doing.

You cannot maintain lockdown status for extended periods, but it might increase your ability to focus.

Chapter 28

The Reluctant Subject Matter Expert

Writing is the act of transferring thoughts from our own brains to those of other people, through words. It's tough enough to marshal your *own* thoughts into coherent order. What happens when you have to extract ideas from other people's brains?

At work, the research process often entails interviewing or speaking with experts on the subject you're writing about. Getting an expert opinion or quote is easy. Sometimes, however, your primary research resides in someone else's head.

This person is now a gating factor in your ability to get the job done. If they don't have the time or inclination to provide the content, you're stuck.

Here are a few ideas for working in this situation.

Getting on the Schedule

Time is precious; to remain in good standing with the expert, make sure you use as little of their time as possible. If this is your first interaction with this person, they may look at you and see a potential time drain. You have to prove yourself.

Before you reach out:

Create the document plan. Understand your objective, audience, and reader's reason. Communicate exactly what you need from the expert and why.

Do other research. Find out as much as possible ahead of time, so you can be an informed and receptive audience. If you are writing about an internal project, ask for email threads. Prepare a few questions in advance to get the conversation rolling. Ask for anything they can provide in advance of the meeting. For example, "Do you have any design documents or email threads that would be useful for me to read ahead of time?"

Scope and communicate the time commitment. Having done the work, you should have a good understanding of how much time you might need. "Can you give me thirty minutes this week to talk about a blog post I'm writing on your project?"

The Preferred Communication Method

People frequently assume that you want *them* to write when you ask for help with a writing project.

For some people, writing comes naturally. Others (who haven't read this book) may shrink from the task and put you off. Be clear about what you expect.

Find out how the source would prefer to interact with you, and work with them in their preferred method.

- *In person*: It's often easiest to meet with the person to discuss the topic and take notes.
- *On the phone*: Ask permission to record the call so you can focus on the discussion rather than taking notes.
- *In writing*: If the source would rather write, ask for a list of key points to cover or any existing notes. Make it clear that you will outline and draft based on the content, rather than using exactly what they deliver.

For technical experts not comfortable with these options, consider using the whiteboard technique.

The Magic of the Whiteboard

For many years, I made my living working in the geekiest intersections of technology and marketing. I dove deep into the application stack or hacked through forests of terminology and abstraction to find the business value in topics such as domain naming infrastructure, email certification, and storage virtualization.

My secret? I knew the magic of the whiteboard.

I'd request a one-on-one conversation with the key person involved in the project, often a developer, Chief Technology Officer, or system architect. I'd ask them to sit with me for thirty to sixty minutes and do a "core dump" about the topic. In the software context, a core dump happens when a computer writes the contents of its memory to a file as a debugging aid. Using this term made it clear that I did not expect anyone to write down or organize thoughts unless they wanted to. I would make sense of whatever they spit out.

We would find a room with a whiteboard. Marker in hand, my contact drew boxes and wrote labels, and the words then started flowing. The speaker turned back and forth between the board and me. I'd ask a question; they'd check in to see if I was following. It all happened naturally, like a conversation, but with the comfort and security of the whiteboard.

This strategy takes pressure off the person with the content in their heads. They don't have to rely on words alone; they can draw boxes to make connections or illustrate concepts on the board. They don't have to present information in a linear manner, but can skip around between areas, drilling down when it makes sense.

Most people are happy to explain things to an interested, attentive audience, and happier still if you don't ask them to write.

The Prototype Strategy

Sometimes you cannot get *any* advance attention from the subject matter expert. In this case, give them a prototype to criticize and pull apart, so you can determine what they're thinking.

Many people cannot envision the finished product. They find it easier to comment on an existing document. Put together a quick prototype based on the best information available and your project plan.

This strategy appears to contradict my earlier advice to plan carefully and get approvals before you start writing. In certain situations, writing first is the only way to spur someone into providing the necessary insight.

The key to this strategy is not to invest too much energy or effort in the prototype, so you don't waste your time polishing things that will only disappear. Follow these three guidelines:

1. Only prototype the sections for which you need input from the source.
2. Set expectations by telling the expert that this document is just a prototype, awaiting their guidance. Give it a label like "working draft" or "straw man."
3. Distribute it only to the people from whom you need content. You don't want to inadvertently kick off the review and approval cycle before you're ready.

Overcoming Resistance

A technology company once hired me to rework its web copy and create several papers for a business audience.

The Chief Technology Officer for the company was a prominent writer, blogger, and thought leader in the industry. He was an excellent writer when creating content for a technical audience.

Unfortunately, his lengthy papers were not accessible for the average reader, including investors and business decision makers. With such a deep understanding of his technical domain, he suffered from the curse of knowledge.

In our first team meeting to kick off the writing projects, it quickly became clear that he was *not* happy about the company hiring a writer. He came right out and said it.

Uh-oh. This was the guy I needed to work with, and he didn't think I should be there.

I don't know the source of his resistance. Perhaps he disagreed with the executive who hired me. It might have been part of a power struggle within the company. Rather than spending time speculating, I focused on finding the right way to collaborate with this individual.

My best advice for a situation like this is as follows:

Do your homework. I had already read several of his blog posts before the meeting; afterward, I dove into the lengthy papers he'd written. I found as much as possible in those documents that I could use so that he wouldn't feel like he was revisiting issues he'd already written about.

Be professional. I couldn't take his feelings personally—I had a job to do for the reader. Getting defensive would have been the worst reaction in this situation.

Advocate for the reader. Take the focus off who is "right" and puts it instead on the reader's needs. Doing this puts political intrigue and disagreements in the background, and changes the conversation from the past to the future.

I created rough, prototype copy based on his developer-oriented content and his answers to my questions. He made extensive revisions, which then became the first drafts. Pretty quickly, we established an effective, collaborative relationship.

In the end, he felt a sense of ownership in the results, without having to spend much of his time on the content. He remained firmly at the helm of the company's technical direction, while ceding control of the way this message was packaged for a broader audience. Focusing on the needs of the readers ultimately won the day.

Chapter 29

The Shrinking Deadline

Our heroes are trapped in a room when they realize the walls are slowly closing in. Each passing moment brings them closer to a terrifying, crushing end. The tension mounts, tempers fray.

You've seen this concept many times, whether in the old *Batman* television series or in the movie *Star Wars, A New Hope*. (There's a movie based solely on this premise, called *Fermat's Room*.)

Even if it's campy, the scene makes me squirm every time. Maybe that's because as a writer, it hits too close to home.

In software projects, when the development deadlines slip but the ship date doesn't move, *somebody* gets squeezed. Often, the writer is stuck with less and less room to maneuver, becoming trapped in the shrinking deadline room.

People who buy into the One-Step Writing Myth don't worry about sacrificing writing time. They believe that writing should take exactly as long as required to put the requisite number of words down in a file. What's the problem with stealing a day or two from the writing phase?

We know better.

What can you do if you're stuck in the shrinking deadline room? Here are ideas for adapting your processes to deal with the crunch-time deadlines.

Start planning early. Resist the temptation to wait until everything is ready to start work. With careful planning, you can invest time up front to make the deadline easier to deal with.

Identify the key people and lay out the review and approval strategy beforehand. "Since time will be tight, let's clarify how we're going to get this through approvals now. We'll only have time for one review cycle. Lee will have final say on the legal issues, Joan on accuracy of the content, and Max on strategy. I've got final approval on editorial issues."

This is also a great time to invoke the "opt-in" revision clause: "I will send you the review draft on Monday the 21st. Please plan to make time to look at it promptly. If I don't hear from you by 5pm on Wednesday, the 23rd, I'll assume you approve."

Making these decisions before starting to write streamlines the approval process. In addition, these messages subtly remind others that you are "taking one for the team" and working to a tight schedule. That can't hurt.

Research and incubate. If you don't have the details yet, start researching and outlining with the content available, so you can set your brain to incubating the ideas you will need to write.

Write in shifts. It might be possible to write parts of the final product before you have everything you need. If so, create a working outline and draft sections you feel confident will be needed.

Use parallel processing. Once you finally are free to work on the project, enlist other people to support you. Get a person you trust to edit and revise your work while you write the next sections. Ask for proofreading or editorial assistance.

Create the minimum viable document first. A friend of mine writes technical documentation for software products and must wait for the engineers to finish their work before she has the necessary details. "In products with a graphical user interface, the last part of the code to change is the user interface and online messages. Unfortunately, that's the part I need for documentation."

She focuses on creating the minimum viable document, working from general content to the specifics. She creates a document that covers everything at a high level, and then drills down, bit by bit, as she has time and access to the project. She resists diving deep into one section until she knows that everything is covered. At any point, she could ship the document and it would work.

Think of yourself as an artist painting a canvas. Sketch the outline, then gradually add details, always making sure you can see the entire picture.

Stage the reviews. If you can write in phases, you might be able to send parts of the document out for reviews or approvals. If you need a sign-off on one specific section, send it out while you're writing another.

This strategy works well if you suspect that one part of a project is likely to incur the most discussion. Draft that section first and get it out to the people with approval or review status.

When the time comes for the final review process, you can let people know what's happened: "Legal has already signed off on the section about partnerships."

Communicate the trade-offs. Let people know the adjustments you are making, and ask for resources (editing, proofing, layout, etc.) so that you can meet the deadline.

Writing is a team endeavor. Step up and do your part in a crisis, but use the planning process to communicate that this is a one-time situation—not the new normal.

Chapter 30

Collaborative Writing

Although writing in the workplace is a team sport, usually only *one* team member bats at a time. After the planning phase, the designated writer accepts responsibility for putting the words together for the first draft.

In some situations, however, team participation also extends to the drafting phase. Truly collaborative writing presents significant challenges for all participants. Have a clearly defined plan and adjust it as you work. Before you decide how to collaborate, understand why you're doing it.

Examine the Motives

Group writing projects typically arise from one of the following three situations:

1. Assigning multiple stakeholders to the writing process to satisfy internal politics (writing by committee)
2. Adding writers to accelerate the output (writing in parallel)

3. Creating content that is the unique result of several individuals working together (true collaboration)

In the first situation, writing by committee, everyone's pet ideas or phrases get a chance to be heard (or removed) during negotiated drafting. The process is subject to the perils of *groupthink*, a kind of dysfunctional group decision making that arises from our natural desire to achieve consensus and avoid conflict. The resulting text may check the boxes of all the committee members, but rarely serves the reader's needs. Avoid it if possible.

> Writing by committee is painful. True collaboration is fulfilling.

The second situation, adding writers to speed the end result, often happens on massive projects. Depending on the project, this strategy may *add* as much time in planning and revision as it saves in drafting.

In the famous book about programming, *The Mythical Man-Month*, author Fred Brooks Jr. debunks the idea that adding programmers to a project accelerates it: "Adding manpower to a late software project makes it later." The same thing can happen with writing.

To accelerate a project or reduce the load on an author, consider adding collaborators in *other* phases of the project, including research, revision and editing, and review management.

The third reason to write as a team is to generate better or different content than any participant could achieve individually.

This kind of collaboration requires a trusting relationship. Each writer must be willing to work in service of the end result.

Collaboration Models

Collaborative authorship is a difficult balance to maintain. Much will depend on your ability to work with the others on the team. Determine which model works for your team.

One writer, multiple authors: In this model, the group might work closely together determining the objectives, researching, and creating the outline. The group discusses the key points of each section verbally or in written communications. The designated writer (who may also contribute content) assembles the words into a draft, which the team revises together.

Multiple writers as one voice: Some coauthors divide the work, each writing certain sections and then assembling them as one. An editor can create a consistent tone and style at the end. This kind of collaboration requires careful division of work and ongoing communication so that the reader experiences a consistent flow.

Multiple writers in an anthology: In this case, you do not attempt to disguise the reality of multiple writers. You still need to collaborate closely to be sure that the finished work serves the reader's interests. Work together planning the objectives, creating an outline, and making key decisions about tone and style.

Determine ahead of time how you are going to work out potential conflicts about content, style, and tone. For example, a subject matter expert might collaborate with a professional writer to draft a book; the writer should have the say on tone and style, and the expert on the content matter.

Many wonderful films, books, and television shows are the results of successful, productive collaboration. If you have a chance to work on a writing team, set out with clear expectations and roles, and a commitment to the reader. True collaboration may be an opportunity for growth.

Chapter 31

Recognition and Attribution

The work of planning, scoping, revising, and managing approvals described in this book is invisible to most people. They don't see the effort behind the scenes, only the finished product. Good writers make the process look easy.

The nature of the work often requires that you, as the writer, disappear. You may be ghostwriting or creating content in the brand voice. Your name doesn't show up on the final product. The more effective you are, the less you are seen in the written work.

Writers in this situation may feel unappreciated or unacknowledged. Remember the unappreciated writers from the Introduction? They may feel resentful about not having authorship.

While joy in the work is lovely, acknowledgment is also important. We are social animals and want to be valued.

Your voice might disappear in the work, but don't disappear in your job.

Authorship, Attribution, and Recognition

As a workplace writer, you may have to cede authorship of the documents you write. You invest effort in the work and planning, but another person's name goes in the byline.

That's the nature of the job.

Attribution is particularly elusive in scientific or technical fields. One writer I know who worked with engineers on technical documents described his situation this way:

"The engineer provided raw and usually badly written material … The final product never looked like the raw material provided. Yet the he would want to claim authorship."

The engineer probably believed in the Big Idea Myth: that writing is mostly about the ideas, while execution is trivial. You and I know better, but we won't be able to convince the entire world.

Further, it may be in the organization's interest that the engineers, senior staff, or executives claim authorship. Authorship makes these individuals appear like thought leaders, benefiting the business that employs them.

If it pains you to be slaving away as an unwilling ghost-writer, remember that authorship isn't everything. Recognition comes in many guises:

- *Authorship* credit or a *byline* signals to the external world that you contributed ideas to a piece of content. In academic journals, the order in which names are listed is theoretically proportional to the contribution, or to the seniority and importance of the contributors. For example, in the following attribution, Jane as-

sumes more credit than John: By Jane Doe and John
Smith.

- *Attribution* is a public record of your role in a project.
  When seeing the following byline, most people assume
  that John did the writing: By Jane Doe with John
  Smith.

- *Acknowledgment* is recognition of your effort, within
  your team, organization, or the world at large. When
  the Apple Macintosh first shipped with Apple software, you could click the *About the Software* menu op-
  tion and see the list of developers who authored it.
  Apple gave external recognition to people who usually
  remained hidden behind the code.

These are the levels of recognition that you have to work
with. Negotiate for the best you can get.

Don't Cling to Authorship

Remember, your dual obligations are to the reader (you are an
advocate) and the business (you are part of a team). If you are
a ghostwriter, embrace it. Effective ghosting is a skill.

If you don't see yourself in this role, you can end up in a
difficult, adversarial relationship with your coworkers. That
attitude impedes collaboration and jeopardizes the work.

One of the proudest moments in my consulting career
was contributing an article to *Dr. Dobb's Journal* on behalf of a
client's Chief Technology Officer (CTO) about a fairly technical topic. *Dr. Dobb's Journal* was an uber-techie publication
for software developers. When the magazine printed an article I'd submitted with the CTO's byline, I was delighted. It

was a sign that I'd successfully mastered the developer's perspective.

The people who mattered to me knew that I'd written it: the bylined executive and others at the company, including the person who paid me. That was enough.

Acknowledgment

Without attribution or public acknowledgment, make sure that people who know your work understand what you have done.

> Be visible where it matters.

Make the process visible to those around you. ("I'm in the research phase for x, and drafting for y.") If you take ownership of the planning process and communicate through reviews, people will realize the depth of your contribution.

Include the work you wrote for someone else in your list of completed projects for your team. ("I wrote four blog posts for the CFO.")

Bonus: When listing completed projects, include the impact the project had on the business at large, if possible. Consider whether it contributed to visibility, customer loyalty, or any other business-wide impact.

Here are a few examples of articulating your impact.

- I wrote a technology brief about the new feature after the customer success group told us people weren't using it yet. They've started sending the brief out today, and I'll check in next week to see if it's inspiring customers to try the feature.

- I wrote four blog posts for the CFO. *CFO* magazine published one of them. That post has been shared 300 times so far.

- I wrote a blog post about next week's webinar. The social media team spread the word, and we picked up 100 registrations the day that post was published.

The reader doesn't have to know who you are. What matters is that you are successful and valued in your organization.

Resources for Successful Workplace Writers

Now I've shared with you the secrets of my writing career. Perhaps calling them *secrets* is overstating the case. Many of the practices seem commonsense or obvious.

Plan before you write? Identify the audience? Revise from the top down?

Yet they weren't all obvious to me when I set out in my writing career. I learned many of them the hard way. And as we know from pilots and their checklists, writing down the obvious steps can protect you from failures.

This section gives you a few tools to turn my hard-earned lessons into standard operating procedures on your job, such as:

- Checklists you can use or modify to establish your own processes—ensuring that the work you do moves smoothly from start to completion.
- A sample worksheet for planning, scoping, and scheduling your work. Try it out, track your time, and become a master of planning and scheduling writing tasks.

It also includes a listing of additional resources, as well as those cited in this book, so you can continue to explore the ideas covered here.

This doesn't have to be the end. Visit AnneJanzer.com and sign up for my Writing Practices list; you'll receive weekly updates and suggestions about writing productivity, creativity, and effectiveness. Or send me questions and suggestions using the Contact form on that site.

What you do now is up to you. I hope you're well on your way to doing more writing and becoming a valued, successful writer in your workplace and beyond.

The Checklists

Checklists protect you from skipping essential steps, while creating a structure for team communications.

Here are sample checklists for each phase of the project plan. Use or adapt them for your own purposes. Download PDF and spreadsheet versions of these checklists from AnneJanzer.com/WWP.

Planning Checklist

Before you set out to write, make sure you have agreement on these items.

1. **Objective**
   - Macro: Big picture purpose
   - Micro: What you want the reader to do
2. **Audience**
3. **Reader's reason:** Why does the reader care?

4. **Format**

- What is it (paper, post, etc.)
- How will people read it (online, print)
- Approximate length (words or pages)
- Repurposing (what else can it become?)

5. **Review process**

- Reviewers
- Approvers

6. **Schedule**

- Content-creation deadline
- Review deadline
- Final approval deadline
- Publication deadline

Revision Checklist

Whether you use one revision pass or four, use the following list to make sure you've checked everything.

First revision pass

- ✓ The piece meets its main objective
- ✓ The introduction pulls the reader in
- ✓ The headings and subheadings make sense

Second pass

- ✓ It flows well start to finish
- ✓ Unfamiliar or unknown abstractions are defined

Third pass

- ✓ Grammar and spelling check
- ✓ Tone and style match corporate style

Proofreading

   ✓ You have checked the piece in its final format

Review/Approval Checklist

Use the following checklist to guide your review and approval processes.

1. **Planning**
   - ✓ Identify reviewers
   - ✓ Identify approvers
   - ✓ Create a schedule
   - ✓ (Bulletproof) Decide review authority in advance (who weighs in on what)
   - ✓ (Bulletproof) Send outline and objectives to review before writing

2. **Asking for reviews**
   - ✓ State the review objective
   - ✓ Set an explicit deadline
   - ✓ Reminder reviewers 24 hours ahead

3. **Acting on review**
   - ✓ Integrate comments
   - ✓ Manage any conflicts

4. **Final sign-off**
   - ✓ Send to approvers
   - ✓ Integrate final feedback if necessary

Scoping and Scheduling the Work

Accurate project scoping and scheduling are skills developed over time. The first step is to create a plan, then track how you execute on it. If you do this for several projects, you'll start to discover trends.

These are the key steps to approaching the scheduling and scoping process:

1. Break the work into its component phases
2. Determine the effort time required for each phase.
3. From that, come up with a calendar (elapsed) time longer than the effort time, leaving room for incubation.
4. If you have a final due date, start with that and work backward to determine calendar deadlines.

If possible, add a 20 percent buffer to the combined research, outline, drafting, and revision, because one of those parts will take longer than you anticipate.

Use the following as a template. (You can also download a spreadsheet to modify from AnneJanzer.com/WWP.)

Phase	Effort Time	Calendar Time	Deadline
Planning			
Research			
Outline			
Drafting (2 passes, incubation)			
Revision			
External review			
Integrating review comments			
Approval (if separate)			
Final publication prep			

Further Reading and Notes

Suggested Reading

Below are some of the books that I consulted when writing *The Workplace Writer's Process* and while refining my own practices. All are worthwhile additions to a writer's library.

The Checklist Manifesto: How to Get Things Right, by Atul Gawande (Metropolitan Books). Gawande presents compelling benefits of the humble checklist, with stories from medicine, aviation, and construction. You'll want to start making checklists.

Creativity: Flow and the Psychology of Discovery and Invention, by Mihaly Csikszentmihalyi (HarperCollins). Csikszentmihalyi surveys artists, scientists, writers, and others responsible for creative breakthroughs to understand the processes behind creativity.

Everybody Writes: Your Go-To Guide to Creating Ridiculously Good Content, by Ann Handley (Wiley). This book offers terrific guidance on writing and revising in the business context. Plus, it's an entertaining read.

Flow: The Psychology of Optimal Experience, by Mihaly Csikszentmihalyi (Harper Perennial). This is the essential guidebook to the state of flow, from the psychologist who has studied it most deeply. It's also a philosophical work.

Grit: The Power of Passion and Perseverance, by Angela Duckworth (Scribner). Significant achievement in nearly any field requires persistent effort. This book offers strategies for developing your own grit.

The Language Instinct: How the Mind Creates Language, by Steven Pinker (Harper Perennial). The author dives into the alignment of language and thought processes, combining cognitive science and linguistics.

The Mythical Man-Month: Essays on Software Engineering, by Frederick P. Brooks Jr. (Addison-Wesley). This book has been guiding software engineers for decades; if you work in the software field, check it out. Some of its advice relates well to writers.

The Myths of Creativity: The Truth About How Innovative Companies and People Generate Great Ideas, by David Burkus (Jossey-Bass). Burkus exposes common myths about creativity that get us into trouble.

Purple Cow: Transform Your Business by Being Remarkable, by Seth Godin (Portfolio). I'd recommend nearly anything by Seth Godin for anyone interested in business communications and marketing. *Purple Cow* is a great starting point.

The Sense of Style: The Thinking Person's Guide to Writing in the 21st Century, by Steven Pinker (Viking). As its title suggests, this book is filled with detailed advice for the writer, based on how our readers process what we write. It also includes the best grammar explanations I've ever seen.

Thinking, Fast and Slow, by Daniel Kahneman (Farrar, Straus and Giroux). The layperson's guide to behavioral economics, it's densely packed with insight into the way we think and decide.

Notes from the Text

Chapter 1: Angela Duckworth's quote about the naturalness bias can be found on page 25 of her book *Grit: The Power of Passion and Perseverance.*

Chapter 4: Steven Pinker's quote about the curse of knowledge appears on page 61 of *The Sense of Style: The Thinking Person's Guide to Writing in the 21ˢᵗ Century.*

Chapter 6: The quote about checklists is found on page 48 of Atul Gawande's *The Checklist Manifesto: How to Get Things Right.*

Chapter 11: You can find examples of Marc Andreessen's tweetstorms on the Andreessen Horowitz website at a16z.com/tag/tweetstorms.

Chapter 17: Many biographers have written about Monet. My source was the book *Mad Enchantment: Claude Monet and the Painting of the Water Lilies,* by Ross King. The quote about layering is from *Writing to Deadline: The Journalist at Work,* by Donald M. Murray.

Chapter 30: The quote about the dangers of adding programmers to a late software project can also be found in *The Mythical Man-Month.*

Acknowledgments

If you want proof that writing *is a team* sport, look no further. This book is indebted to a large roster of talented contributors, coaches, cheerleaders, and others.

Many individuals have lobbed ideas and content my way to add to the book. These players include Christina Procopiou, Christine Goodner, Ann McCowan, Stephan Hovnanian, Robert Hubbard, Maria Ross, and Karen Catlin.

Ellen Pifer introduced me to the Adobe Enterprise Writers group, a wonderful team itself that contributed invaluable advice.

I also owe a debt to the many client teams that I've worked with as a writer over the years. Many of those clients supported me as I figured out all the practices in this book, and have now become long-term colleagues and friends. There's no better argument for developing effective processes than the fact that it frees you to collaborate with people like

Lisa Abbott, Randy Brasche, Tom Hogan, Carol Broadbent, Jim Nisbet, Jon Brody, and so many others. You know who you are. This book would not be here without those clients and friends.

Other people have served as coaches in this book publishing adventure, including Holly Brady and Chris Syme.

A few people keep showing up to cheer me on and support me through multiple books, including Roger C. Parker, Douglas Burdett, David Meerman Scott, Linda Popky, David Burkus, and Ann Handley.

My coaching clients provide ongoing inspiration and incentives, helping me think more deeply about my own writing processes.

Laurie Gibson and Mark Rhynsburger make sure I adhere to the rules of the game with their incredible editing and proofreading prowess. Any mistakes that remain are mine alone.

The wonderful people who subscribe to my Writing Practices list offer feedback on ideas as I bounce them out, giving me something to look forward to as I assemble posts for them each week.

Closer to home, my children, Emily and Mark, offer moral support as well as their insights into programming and productivity. All of my books owe a great deal to my husband Steve's invaluable insight, ongoing support, audio engineering skills, and unending patience.

About the Author

Anne Janzer is a writing coach, author, and recovering marketer. She enjoys working with writers, talking about writing, and writing books.

The Writer's Process: Getting Your Brain in Gear combines the lessons of a writing career with the teachings of cognitive science to uncover the secrets of writing productivity. The book won the Foreword Reviews INDIES Book of the Year 2016 Silver Medal for writing.

Subscription Marketing: Strategies for Nurturing Customers in a World of Churn helps marketers navigate the disruptions of the subscription economy. That book is now in its second edition and being translated into Japanese.

Anne has worked with over a hundred technology businesses, from industry giants to innovative start-ups, helping them articulate positioning and messaging in crowded markets.

Her work as a ghostwriter for corporate executives has appeared in dozens of industry publications and blogs, including Wired.com and the Sand Hill blog. In her own name, she contributes to numerous industry and corporate blogs. Find out what she's up to next on her website, AnneJanzer.com.

Index

CPSIA information can be obtained
at www.ICGtesting.com
Printed in the USA
LVOW13s2159310718
585553LV00027B/440/P